Marianne Svärd Häggvik

RUSTIC

GARDEN PROJECTS

STEP-BY-STEP BACKYARD DÉCOR FROM TRELLISES TO TREE SWINGS, STONE STEPS TO STAINED GLASS

TRANSLATED BY ANETTE CANTAGALLO

SKYHORSE PUBLISHING

Contents

Photos from left to right:
Shady resting spot p 19, citrus support p 231,
suet ball bird feeder p 179, frog p 45

The Garden
—A Place Where Creativity Thrives

The Dream of an Oasis

I've always liked to make things with my hands and to create and realize ideas. Learning new skills and new techniques opens new worlds. A good way to try your hand at a new craft is to enroll in a course. Usually, you can learn the basics and maybe even make a unique object over a weekend. You don't need to be an expert. Curiosity and dedication go a long way. To me, the garden is a place for enjoyment and relaxation, but also a place where my creativity thrives. In a dream garden, the scrubby corner becomes a green oasis. I realized my dream of beautiful white birch bark by making a simple birch sapling screen that brightens the house's north side. See how it turned out on page 89.

Inspiration from Many Places

Not many garden-people leave unchanged after a visit to lavish private gardens, the species-diverse Kew Gardens, or the mysterious hanging gardens of Ninfa. At places like this, there is always something interesting and useful you can bring to your own garden. To begin with, a garden needs several different elements to become enjoyable and to function properly. The floor may consist of grass or stone. Hedges and trellises form the walls. The roof is created from pergolas and tree crowns. To name a few projects, you will find in this book how to create personal screens, walkways, and plant supports as well as furniture and decorations. Many of the projects are quick and simple, others are more demanding—but the love for the material is what they all have in common. The contrast of stained glass and shiny metal against rough concrete and rusty iron is absolutely lovely. In addition to the base elements, it's exciting to add eye-catchers that surprise or delight. An eye-catcher is just what it sounds like, something that catches the eye. The book's beach stone compass rose and stained glass citrus support are some of the eye-catchers in my garden. If you want to see what these look like, go to pages 127 and 231.

The Plants Play the Lead Role

Many of my favorite plants are included in the project's planting sketches. Some of them have been raised from seeds. Some of them were purchased fully grown. Others have come to me in different ways. The plants with a provenance are my beloved ones. Ingbritt's bright pink "Moving" geranium or Olle's red Christmas rose reminds of my former neighbors. The plant that holds the closest place to my heart is my grandfather's lilies of the valley. Grandpa was my best childhood friend. He skied with me through the forest in the winter and made me willow pipes in the spring. When Grandpa turned fifty in 1945, the neighbors congratulated him with a large basket filled with plants—including blooming lilies of the valley. It was an amazing gift to get on February 27—in the middle of the war and in the middle of the coldest winter. How was it possible? Mom nursed them carefully, and in the spring she planted them in the garden. When I left home, I was given some lilies of the valley to accompany me to the community garden. Today, nearly seventy years after my grandfather's fiftieth birthday party, the lilies are forming a low green carpet beside the romantic ruins on page 163. I love them and immensely enjoy their small, fragrant flowers.

My hope is that this book will give you both inspiration and pleasure, but will also provide clear step-by-step instructions for all kinds projects to adorn your garden.
Warmest good luck!

"Today, nearly seventy years after my grandfather's fiftieth birthday party, the lilies are forming a low green carpet by the romantic ruins on page 163."

CHAPTER Nº1

BRAIDED WILLOW

The Docile Willow

Braiding willow is something everyone can enjoy. In order to create a beautiful plant support, all you need is a few boughs, pruning shears, and a bit of grip strength. It's fascinating to see how the vines can be shaped into fine knots and lovely cable patterns without breaking. The Japanese square knot is beautiful, and it looks difficult to tie; however, once you learn how, it's actually quite simple. Find inspiration from the projects in this chapter and let your willow plant support take shape piece by piece. Once you have the required material available, it only takes a few hours to braid a large trellis or a cone.

The beautiful moon gate by Christian Erlandsson at Yasuragi Hasseludden in Saltsjö-Boo, east of Stockholm. Here, the willow has been braided around a steel frame.

The willow symbolizes perseverance and patience. According to the Taoist religion, the willow is the opposite of spruce and oak. They resist the storm and break, while the willow bends over, only to rise up again when the storm has subsided.

Willow Pieces in the Garden

Willow is a natural material that is easy to handle and blends in well with the garden environment. Even in the simplest constructions, willow gives plants great support. The more advanced pieces made of willow are almost their own works of art.

The willow has long and thin shoots that grow 3–4 m in a summer. They are flexible and pliable, and these unique features make them suitable for braiding. For garden projects, mainly the thin and yellow-green one-year or two-year shoots are used. The two-year shoots are thicker and yellowish-brown colored, and can be used to make fences.

Willow and wicker are both available in many colors, including yellow, blue, gray, and red. The shoots suitable for braiding are called "wickers" or "poles" and you can use either fresh or dried willow. Willow is called "green" when it is fresh, and "brown" when dried.

Pick or Purchase Willow?

Fresh willow is available for purchase in the spring or early summer. Willow trees in parks and along avenues are usually pollarded every other year, and you can use the opportunity to collect the trimmed shoots. Some garden organizations arrange willow harvest days during the spring. There, you get to pick willow at farms that grow *Salix* as an energy crop. If you don't have the opportunity to harvest, you can simply purchase willow. Many growers sell *Salix* for gardening.

Freshly harvested willow can be used for a few weeks after it has been cut. Keep it slightly moist and store in the shade. It will retain the moisture longer if it is wrapped in a tarp. Growers keep willow refrigerated, which makes it possible to store it for longer, and they can sell fresh willow throughout the summer.

Dried willow can be purchased throughout the year from places that host willow braiding courses. The rods are sorted by type and length.

Soften Dried Willow

Willow that has been dried must be soaked before it can be used. Since it takes time to get them soft and pliable, it's best to allow the longer twigs to lie soaked in water for up to one week or more. If you live close to a lake, you can drain them in the water by the shore. You can also dig a ditch and put them

A willow twig must be smooth and bendable to be suitable for braiding.

The dry willow twigs soften when soaked in a tarp.

in a large tarp. Then fill the tarp with water and add some weights so the twigs stay under water. The soak time varies depending on the thickness of the twigs and the temperature of the water. If you want to speed up the process, you can put the willow in hot water.

Time to Start Braiding

You can make trellises, screens, fences, and flower supports from soaked dried willow. Fresh willow can be used in the same way, but it can also create living structures.

If you stick a fresh willow rod in the ground, it can develop roots

Plant Facts

Willow, pussy willow, and sallow belong to the plant genus *Salix*, which consists of about 400 species. They are deciduous and grow as trees, shrubs, rods, or mini shrubs. Male and female flowers grow on separate plants. The *Salix* group belongs to the willow plant family Salicaceae, to which poplar and aspen also belong.

In the past, people chewed sallow bark to relieve headaches. It contains salicylic acid, which is still a component in some painkillers today.

and start to grow. It looks delightful as a hut or a fence. If you want the willow rods to develop roots, trim a couple of centimeters from the end and let them stand in a bucket filled with water for a few days before planting. The willow is a thirsty plant and has strong root growth. In a fence or some other smaller construction of living willow that is regularly trimmed, the roots can grow up to a yard in length.

Large willows shouldn't be planted too close to the house since their water-seeking roots could penetrate foundations and underground pipes, and cause damage to both the building's foundations and drainage system. However, a beautiful hanging willow by the shore or pond is a delight.

Considerations

If you use fresh willow as a stay inserted in the ground, it's likely that it will start to develop roots—even if that was not your intention. However, this is easy to fix. If the willow starts to grow leaves, jerk the stay up and down to loosen the delicate, early roots.

Another thing to consider when braiding willow is that fresh willow shrinks up to twenty percent when it dries. Therefore, braid as tight as possible and always leave room for shrinkage. This prevents the braid from becoming too loose and therefore slipping, or the joints loosening when the willow dries.

Other Braiding Materials

It's also possible to braid materials other than willow. Small branches, such as reeds and roots can be used. The key is that the material is flexible and bendable. Experiment and braid with dogwood, hazel, rowan, lime, larch, poplar, and forsythia. They can become a great feature in a willow braid. But to make it simple, I have only used willow of different thicknesses in the projects in this chapter.

Maintenance

A piece made of dried willow will be completely maintenance-free once it is finished. Willow ages beautifully, and the fence will serve its purpose and decorate the place for years to come. The weakest point in a piece made of dried willow is the sticks that are depressed into the ground. After a few years of decay, they might break.

To extend the lifespan significantly, use reinforcing bar instead of willow for the vertical struts that are to be inserted into the ground.

Large amounts of snow are also a danger. There is a great risk that the pressure from the snow will break the brittle willow. If possible, put peony supports and growth cones in a dark and cold storage room during the winter.

Lastly, in the springtime, one may treat the willow-made pieces with boiled linseed oil mixed with equal parts turpentine. This strengthens the willow rods and allows them to hold up a bit longer.

A Brief History

Remains of basketry from about 8000 years BC have been found in the Middle East and Africa. During the Middle Ages (about 500 AD to the 1500s) people braided fences and enclosures of willow to keep cattle in place and to protect crops. Fishermen made creels to catch fish, farmers made harvest baskets, and toddlers slept in braided cradles. The traditional basket-weaving profession still exists and many of the skilled basket makers teach their craft. In fact, all baskets that are sold are made by hand—so far, no machine can braid baskets!

Braiding Methods

The basic principle of braiding willow is simple. Coarser willow rods are used as braces. The distance between the struts depends on the thickness of the braces and the braiding material's thickness. The finer the braiding material is, the denser the strut bars can be positioned. Thinner willow twigs are braided in between the braces. When the first twig is fully braided, you interlace it with a new one and continue braiding. The twigs should be interlaced: tip to tip or butt end to butt end. Let the old and the new twig overlap one or several braces. This gives you a strong and sustainable braid. Cut off the ends at the rear of the strut. Leave at least 1–2 cm for shrinkage. There are many different types of braiding: scissor braiding, French braiding, and chain braiding to name a few. However, when you're getting started, it's not necessary to know all of these braids. If you master simple braiding, scissor braiding, and double crisscross braiding you'll have come a long way.

In simple braiding, you work with one twig at a time. Alternate the twig from the outside to the inside every other time. Simple braiding is perfect for low fences and screens.

Double crisscross braiding is good for making round objects. Here you work with two twigs of equal length and thickness. Start by inserting the thick ends of the two twigs behind nearby braces. Then take the twig on the left and put it in front of the next brace, above the twig on the right, and then behind the next brace. Continue in the same way with the other twig (which has now become the left). Double crisscross braids become denser than simple braids.

A scissor braid is made by bending a twig in half and wrapping it around the outer brace. Then the twig is crossed, or "scissored" between each brace. If the braces stand sparsely, you may need to scissor the twig several times between each brace. Scissor braiding is suitable for making open braids.

Interlace a Twig

Sometimes you'll have the misfortune of a braided twig breaking. If it's positioned in such a way that it's important to the piece's appearance, then it may be worthwhile to fix the problem by interlacing it with a new twig.

1. Cut the willow twig where it broke so it is an even cut. Drill a hole in the middle of the twig and insert a stick into the hole that is just big enough that it fits.

2. Join the twigs.

3. Fold a piece of string to form a 3 cm long loop. Put the loop along the twig, centered over the joint. Wrap the string around the twig and the loop until only a small loop remains. Insert the string through the small loop and cut it off about 3 cm outside the loop.

4. Pinch the string's end with needle-nose pliers and pull the string so that the loop is closed.

5. Continue pulling the string so that the other end is pulled into the knot.

6. Cut the ends that are still sticking out.

Round Willow Pieces

There are different ways to keep in place the willow sticks that will form the body of a round climbing frame.

The easiest way is to insert the rods straight down into the ground so the braided plant stays at the actual site. But if there isn't much space in the flowerbed, it may become a little troublesome to braid.

In this case it may be better to insert the rods into a sandbox or into the lawn while you braid, and then you can move the completed climbing frame to the flowerbed when you're done.

A third option is to use a simple drilling template made of plywood to keep the rods in place. If you insert the rods into a drilling template, you can also braid the climbing frame indoors.

BIRD'S NEST

The arrival of spring—with the warming rays of the sun, spring flowers, and birdsong—is one of the highlights of the year. The energy is flowing, and it's time to decorate our gardens. The most delicious still-lifes, such as a beautiful stone covered with lichen, or a cute little bird's nest, depict nature itself. Obviously, the birds should be left to keep their own carefully braided nests, but you can create one yourself from vines and small twigs. My bird's nest gives that extra bit of flair to this spring's first arrangement, although it is not as well made as a real bird's nest.

MATERIALS

- 4 small, fresh willow twigs
- Dry twigs
- Wild grasses
- 3 stone or concrete eggs

TOOLS

- Pruning shears

STEP BY STEP

You can easily collect materials from the garden and from the nearest willow grove. Wild grasses can be used instead of ornamental grass.

1 Make the nest's brace with fresh willow twigs. First, take two twigs and shape them into a ring. Fold the other two twigs back and forth over the ring so that they form a support for the bottom of the nest. Secure the ends by inserting them between the twigs in the outer ring.

2 Fill out the body by weaving some of the dry birch twigs into the space between the willow twigs. This way, a bottom is formed and the nest becomes much denser.

3 Build the nest's outer wall by braiding birch and dried grass. Line the inside of the nest with grass to make it soft and snuggly. Lastly, add the eggs, and the bird's nest is ready!

Hyacinthus orientalis

SHADY RESTING SPOT

A garden needs many sitting areas. The large terrace to the west is perfect for the summer evening barbecue; the lilac arbor is a cozy spot for the children's party with strawberry cordial and creamy birthday cake. And it's absolutely wonderful to sit on the little bench in the cherry grove when the cherry blossom petals float down like snowflakes against the ground. The shady resting spot is a very special place, created for the summer's hottest days. When the sun is hot and the perspiration flows, it's a relief to lean back against the cool stone in the shade of the trees. Willow twigs have been braided into a mesh to make a sparse background wall.

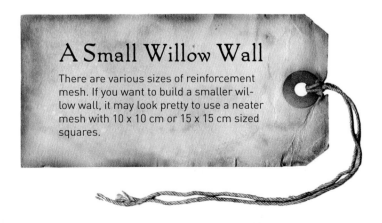

A Small Willow Wall

There are various sizes of reinforcement mesh. If you want to build a smaller willow wall, it may look pretty to use a neater mesh with 10 x 10 cm or 15 x 15 cm sized squares.

MATERIALS

- 1 stone for the backrest (approx. 40 x 60 cm)
- 1–2 stones for a footrest (30 x 50 cm and 20 x 30 cm)
- 4–6 stones that support the seat and the back support (at least 15 x 15 x 15 cm)
- 1 wooden plank (50 x 400 x 1330 mm)
- 3 impregnated fence posts, each 2.2 m (5 cm)
- 1 reinforcement mesh with 20 x 20 cm squares (155 x 290 cm)
- 24 staples or 24 nails (50 x 2 mm)
- 150 liters of potting soil
- 1 ground cloth or tarpaulin (3.3 x 3.5 m)
- 1 wooden board (3.30 m)
- 0.6 m³ stone ($^{15}/_{80}$)
- Approx. 120 willow twigs, at least 170 cm long

TOOLS

- Marking sticks
- Iron bar
- Sledgehammer
- Spirit level
- Hammer
- Spade
- Scissors
- Pruning shears

PLANTS

- Japanese sedge, *Carex morrowii* "Ice Dance" (2 pcs)
- Snowy Woodrush, *Luzula nivea* (1 pc)

STEP BY STEP

To have lovely, cool stones you need to find a place where the trees provide the most shade for the longest time during the day. I had two leftover reinforcement meshes that I started with. It's best to use a mesh that covers the entire surface.

1 Select a large stone that is suitable as a back rest, a flat stone as a foot rest, and some small rocks of equal height to support the seat.

2 Lay out the seat, foot, and back rests so that you can mark the shape and size of the resting spot with marker pegs.

3 With an iron rod, make a hole in the ground for each fence post. The deeper the hole, the steadier the post will stand.

4 Use a sledgehammer to hit the fence posts down into the soil until they are 1.5 meters in height. Attach the reinforcing mesh to the backs of the posts with staples or nails. Use a spirit level to check that the poles and the mesh are straight.

5 Bend the nail over the rebar so that the reinforcement sits firmly against the post.

6 Peel off the grass inside the resting spot's marked-off area so that the stone surface will be level with the surrounding lawn. Dig pits where the plants will be planted. Each pit should be at least 40 cm wide and 40 cm deep. Fill the pits with rich potting soil.

7 Place a ground cloth or tarpaulin so that it covers the resting spot's surface. Wrap the edge of the cloth around a board. The board should rest against the fence posts. This way, a stopper is formed at the outer edge for the stone gravel that will cover the site.

8 Place the back rest, the seat, and the foot rest according to the sketch on the opposite page. Mark the middle of the planting pits by inserting a marker peg in each pit. Cover the cloth with stone gravel.

9 Braid willow twigs into the steel mesh. It's easier if you have a partner. One can insert the twigs from above and the other can direct the twigs into the reinforcement mesh.

10 By only braiding the willow twigs in certain parts of the reinforcing mesh, you can make a "sparse" wall that protects but that still feels open. We stacked three twigs on top of each other before we switched the direction of the braid.

11 Remove the marker pin from one of the planting pits.

12 Brush away the stone gravel to expose the ground cloth covering the planting hole. Cut the cloth open.

13 Fold back the fabric and fix it temporarily with some heavy stones.

14 Insert the plant and close the cloth back over the soil. Water properly so the roots make proper contact with the soil.

15 Lastly, put the gravel back on top of the cloth surrounding the plant. Plant the other two plants in the same way.

Caring For Ornamental Grass

Both Japanese Sedge and Snowy Woodrush are ornamental grasses that thrive in moist soil in partial shade to full shade. The bright leaf edges on the "Ice Dance," and the white flowers on the Snowy Woodrush are very decorative and light up the shade.

The plant's roots should be moist before planting. Don't plant the ornamental grasses too deep; otherwise they may rot.

The type of ornamental grasses that die in the autumn should keep their wilted leaves during the winter. These protect the plant and facilitate the overwintering. You should only cut these away when the spring comes. Cut the leaves a couple of inches above ground.

Japanese Sedge and Snowy Woodrush are both evergreen so they only need a simple trim in the spring. Cut the leaves that are withered or appear unsightly.

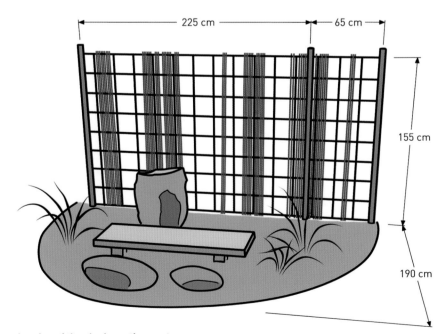

225 cm — 65 cm

155 cm

190 cm

Spec drawing of the shady resting spot

WILLOW BASKET

The entrance to the garden is important in making you and your visitors feel welcome. Although there was vegetation around our gate, it was rather unsatisfying. It needed a warm and welcoming touch. Imagine how nice it would be to be welcomed by a big and beautiful basket filled with seasonal plants. A large basket is also beneficial for other reasons. It can hold a large volume of soil, which provides the plants with good growing conditions, and keeps maintenance needs to a minimum. And if you build the basket with reinforcement bars and willow twigs it will be both durable and pleasant to look at. This basket is anchored in the ground and is stable in all weather conditions.

MATERIALS

- 9 reinforcement bars of approx. 90 cm (10 mm)
- Approx. 120 willow twigs (about 1 cm in diameter)
- 4 m natural fiber string
- 1 black ground cloth (60 x 200 cm)
- 75 liters potting soil

TOOLS

- Bolt cutter
- Ruler
- Protractor
- Scissors
- Sledgehammer
- Pruning shears
- Hacksaw or reciprocating saw

PLANTS

- White *Nicotiana sylvestris* "Only the Lonely" (2 pcs)
- Lime colored red rudbeckia, *Echinacea purpurea* "Coconut Lime" (1 pc)
- White clover, *Oxalis articulata* (2 pcs)
- Coral Bells, *Heuchera sanguinea* "Splendens" (1 pc)

Pot-bound Plants

When a plant's roots have grown far too long in a pot that is too small, the roots press against the container and become tangled and matted. The plant's contact with the soil is reduced; therefore the plant's absorption of nutrients is minimal and the plant fails to thrive. To remedy this, gently invert the pot and loosen the plant. Then trim away the matted roots and loosen the compacted root-ball before re-potting in a new, slightly larger pot with fresh potting soil. The roots will sprout new rootlets and begin to grow out into the new soil instead of continuing to grow in circles. The plant should be watered before and after this operation to minimize shock.

STEP BY STEP

Reinforcement bars are frequently available in lengths of approximately 6 m. Get them precut or cut them yourself with a bolt cutter.

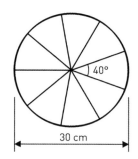

1 Draw a circle of 30 cm diameter on a piece of paper (see p. 230). Divide the circle into nine sections. The vertex of each angle should be 40°.

2 Cut the circle and put it on the ground where the willow basket is to be built. Insert a reinforcement bar in the ground by at the end of each line segment mark.

3 Make sure that all the bars are angled equally so the basket gets an even shape. Strive to make the basket's top edge 50 cm in diameter. Hammer the bars at least 15 cm into the ground.

4 Braid the willow twigs between the bars. Braid one twig at a time; start braiding with the thicker end. Let the twig stick out at least 3–4 cm behind the first bar. Braid the willow in front of the bar every other time and behind the bar every other time.

5 Splice the twigs by placing a new twig so that it overlaps the previous one over two of the bars. Continue braiding the twigs until the basket becomes 55 cm high. With a string, tie the 3 top layers of twigs to each bar.

6 Cut away any ends sticking out around the basket, but keep about one inch of twig (if you cut them too short, the twigs may unravel from the braids as they dry).

7 With a hacksaw or reciprocating saw, cut off the reinforcement bars just above the rim of the basket.

8 Line the inside of the basket with black ground cloth. Let the cloth overlap by 10–20 cm so there won't be any gaps. Fill the basket with good quality potting soil.

9 Before planting, place the plants in a bucket of water so they get properly watered. When no more air bubbles up in the buckets, the plants are ready. This usually takes 2–3 minutes.

10 Plant the flowers in the willow basket and finish off by watering thoroughly so the roots establish contact with the soil.

CLIMBING PLANT TRELLISES

Climbing plants need some kind of growing support so they can climb up toward the light. Dipladenia is a beautiful and colorful plant that quickly grows fiery red flowers and healthy, shiny leaves. It needs a tall trellis to support its long vines. By inserting willow bars into the pot and tying them together with simple and pretty knots, you can make a decorative trellis in less than three hours.

MATERIALS

- 4 willow twigs of 2.5 m (1.5–2 cm in diameter)
- 10 willow twigs of 2.5 m (1 cm in diameter)
- 21 thin willow twigs for braiding (about 0.5 mm in diameter)

TOOLS

- Lopper
- Pruning shears
- Awl

PLANTS

- Dipladenia, *Mandevilla* (1 pc)

Choose the Right Kind of Climbing Plant

Clinging and climbing plants make their way upward using their climbing organs. Some climb with aerial roots, others use adhesive discs, petioles, or tendrils. Dipladenia climbs by twisting its tendrils upward; clematis uses its petioles to fix itself in twists. Both are light, slender plants and are well suited for a plant stay made of willow. Avoid strong-growing, heavy climbing plants. These need a stronger trellis to climb on.

Mandevilla

STEP BY STEP

Start with a climbing plant that has been planted in a pot and build the plant support around it. Direct some tendrils to the willow twigs to make it easier for the plant to start climbing.

1 Insert a long, thick willow twig in each corner of the pot. Push the twig down to the bottom of the pot so it will stand steadily.

2 Then, insert one long, thin willow twig on each side of these corner twigs. Now there should be three willow twigs in each corner of the pot.

3 With a thin willow twig, bundle the three twigs together just above the edge of the pot. Each knot should be tied the same way (see page 36).

4 Insert one long, thin willow twig between two corners of the pot. Bring together the three thin twigs and tie them together 40 cm above the edge of the pot (see illustration A below). Do the same on the opposite side of the pot.

5 Turn the pot 90 degrees. Tie the other two thin corner twigs 60 cm above the edge of the pot (see illustration B below). Do the opposite side in the same way.

6 Turn the pot again. Separate the bound twigs. Tie the two outer twigs to a corner twig 80 cm above the edge (see illustration A below). Do the opposite side in the same way.

7 Tie all the vertical twigs together with scissor braids (see page 14) 120 cm above the pot. Illustrations A and B show which twigs are to be braided.

8 With a coiled knot, fasten the braid to each vertical twig. Save one thin willow twig from each corner. Trim the rest of the twigs an inch above the bonding joints. Lastly, tie together the four thin willow twigs to form a crown on the trellis.

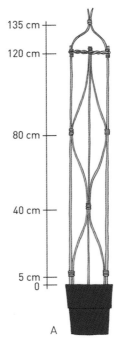

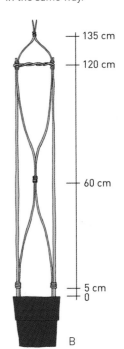

CIRCULAR SWEET PEA PLANT SUPPORT

A summer flower that's hard to do without is the sweet and fragrant sweet pea flower. If you regularly pick the beautiful flowers, you'll be rewarded with continued flowering well into the autumn. The sweet pea shouldn't be allowed to go to seed and form peas; otherwise it will stop flowering. A few plants can provide a full bouquet of flowers every other day during the summer. I like the old-time strong-scented varieties the most. Gentle pastels, clean white, dark purple, or burgundy red sweet peas are all favorites that regularly return to my garden. A circular braided willow plant support is perfect for sweet peas. They'll wind around the willow twigs and quickly fill up the support.

MATERIALS

FOR THE BASE
- 1 piece of masonite (50 cm x 50 cm)

FOR THE PLANT SUPPORT
- 17 willow twigs at least 2.5 m (1.5–2 cm in diameter)
- Approx. 55 willow twigs for braiding (0.5–1 cm in diameter)
- 4 reinforcement bars approx. 1 m (16 mm)
- Cord

TOOLS

- Saw
- Ruler
- Awl
- Cord
- Scissors
- Ruler
- Drill driver
- Drill bit (20 mm)
- Pruning shears
- Small sledgehammer

Lathyrus odoratus

STEP BY STEP

The plant support shouldn't be too sparse. This makes it easier for the plants to climb. The double cross braid is a dense and beautiful braid for making the round support. An odd number of base rods are required. I chose to use seventeen base rods for my sweet pea support.

1 Draw a circle of 36 cm in diameter onto a particle board. Use a bucket or pot of an appropriate size as a template, or use a string to draw the circle (see page 230).

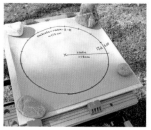

2 Using a ruler, divide the circumference of the circle into seventeen equal parts. A circle with a 18 cm radius has a circumference of about 113 cm. Each segment of the circumference should then measure about 6.65 cm long. Measure and mark the 17 components on the circumference of the circle.

3 Drill holes for the rods at each mark. The base is now complete.

4 Place the drilled base on top of some rocks. Insert the thick willow twigs into the holes to create the frame of the plant support. Let the rods rest against ground. With string, tie the tops of the twigs so they don't fall and separate.

5 Make a border of a double cross braid directly against the surface of the drilled base (see page 14).

6 Splice the twigs for the braiding tip to tip and end to end. Place the twigs so they overlap at the joint. Continue braiding until the border is 12 cm. Finish off the braid by bending the thick end of the last twig at a 90-degree angle and inserting it into the middle of the braid. It should be aligned with the rod so it doesn't stick out.

7 Insert the thick end of a twig to the right of each rod. These will be the decorative twigs between the main rods. Push them down through the braiding all the way to the drilled base. Loosen the string that ties the twigs at the top.

8 Begin the middle border by temporarily tying the first two twigs that are to be braided to the rods, 60 cm above the lower border.

9 Gradually braid the decorative vertical twigs into the border. Place each vertical twig over a vertical rod diagonally to the right. Then, for the last 6 cm set it parallel to the next vertical rod. Braid the border until it is 6 cm tall. Cut the decorative vertical standing twigs 3 cm above the top edge of the border.

10 Braid the upper border at 45 cm above the middle border. It should also be 6 cm tall.

11 Finish the plant support by tying some of the tops of the rods together. Trim every other rod to be approximately 10 cm above the third border, to make it easier to tie together the remaining rods at the top.

12 Tie the rods with a Japanese eye (see page 36) approximately 55 cm above the upper border.

13 Finally, cut the tips of the rods at 20 cm above the Japanese eye.

14 Trim any twig ends that stick out from the braids. Don't cut them too close; leave about an inch so they don't unravel from the braid when the plant support dries.

Vary the Shape

There are many different ways to make a circular plant support. By pulling the rods together before you begin braiding the upper borders, the plant support will become cone shaped. If you press the rods apart instead, the plant support will bulge out and become round at the middle.

15 Hammer four rebars deep into the ground where the plant support will stand. Place the rebars so they directly touch one rod of the plant support.

16 Slip the plant support over the rebars and tie the twigs and rods to the rebars. The support is now firmly anchored to the ground and will be able to remain stable in all weather conditions.

17 Plant the sweet pea seeds directly into the ground or plant pre-cultivated plants when the risk of frost has passed.

FAN TRELLIS

You can never have too many trellises in the garden. They lift the vegetation from the ground and allow for a lot of foliage and greenery while taking up only a very small surface area. A flat willow trellis is perfect to set against a bare and boring wall under the eaves. The trellis is protected there and therefore won't age as fast in the weather. By varying the standing rods' form, you can achieve an entirely different expression with the trellis. At the end of the how-to I've included a version that I call Morticia's trellis. This type of fan-shaped trellis is suitable for summer climbing flowers.

MATERIALS

- 12 willow twigs of 2.5 m (1.5–2 cm in diameter)
- Approx. 50 willow twigs for braiding (1 cm in diameter)
- 5 angle irons (200 x 40 x 40 mm)
- 10 wood screws (4 x 40 mm)
- Cord

TOOLS

- Lopper
- Ruler
- 10 spacer blocks (6 cm wide)
- Pruning shears
- 10 marker sticks
- Awl
- Drill driver
- Drill (3 mm)
- Scissors

PLANTS

- Common morning glory, *Ipomoea purpurea* "Star of Yalta" (5 pcs)

Longevity

The willow twigs will last significantly longer if you place the bottom border of the trellis a bit above ground level so that it is not in contact with the soil. If you have the opportunity to store the trellis indoors during the winter, it will prolong the life of the trellis.

STEP BY STEP

For the vertical rods, select willow twigs that are as equal in thickness as possible. They should also be equal in length, with as few branches at the top as possible. The smoother they are, the easier it will be to create smooth, beautiful arches in the trellis's top edge.

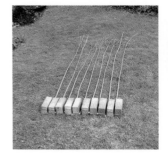

1 Lay the thick twigs on the ground, parallel to each other. Use two-inch-wide concrete blocks to separate each twig. Ensure that the twigs' bottom ends are aligned.

2 The trellis will have two borders of scissor braids (see page 14). Start the first border about 30 cm up from the twigs' bottom ends. Continue the scissor braid until the border becomes 10 cm in height.

3 Now it's time to create the fan shape. Stretch the twigs by sticking the nine marker sticks 1.7 m above the bottom border. Measure with a ruler; the rods should be evenly distributed in a 115 cm-wide fan shape. Insert a new marker stick 30 cm above the middle marker stick as support for the trellis's rounded top edge. Lay one long twig over the new center marker and the two outermost markers to test the rounded shape.

4 Scissor braid the second border 65 cm above the bottom border. Then, lay down two long twigs perpendicularly to the main rods—one above the second border and one below. Let these long twigs stick out at least 10 cm beyond the outer-edge of the trellis.

5 Attach the two perpendicular twigs to every other rod with a Japanese eye (see page 36).

6 Stand right above the rounded top arch. Scissor braid the twigs to the top edge of the trellis. Scissor braid the twigs twice between each rod so the braid becomes sturdy.

7 Make another scissor-braided border and secure the braid to the outer twigs with cross joints (see next spread).

8 Trim the top edge of the scissor braid border, and cut the parallel twigs to be 7 cm beyond the outer edge of the trellis. Trim any twig ends that are sticking out, but allowing space for shrinkage. Trim the top shoots. Of the twig tops, form a central loop and two lateral loops. Insert the top ends in the interstices between the border and rods. If it is too tight, you may have to use an awl.

9 Bend the middle willow rod down and tie it to the rounded arch of the trellis. This gives the top loop a nice shape.

10 Measure where the 5 brackets should be placed on the wall. The bottom rims of the two scissor braid borders should each rest on two brackets. The fifth bracket should be placed so the top edge rests on the iron. Drill the holes and screw-mount the brackets.

11 Hang the trellis on the brackets, and tie the trellis to the brackets' outer edges so it's steady.

Morticia's Trellis

One early spring, I had a stack of freshly harvested willow twigs by my side, when thoughts of the quirky Addams family popped to mind. The black-clad family would pose around Morticia, who sat on a big, beautiful wicker chair. The grand back support inspired me to make this willow trellis. When the trellis was done, I went inside and looked up Morticia's wicker chair, and I discovered that my memory conflicted significantly with reality!

Instructions:
Lay 8 willow twigs on the ground; keep a bit of distance between them. Make two 10 cm-wide scissor braided borders, 25 cm and 60 cm from the bottom. Braid the twigs in a grid pattern and insert a marker stick as support above each crossing point. On both sides of the trellis, braid the narrow ends of two long twigs under the upper border. Bend the twigs so they form a soft, fine shape around the trellis, and fold them together at the trellis's top. Secure the fold with a coiled knot (see page 36). Secure the vertical twigs to the arch with cross knots. Trim any twig ends that stick out.

Decorative Braided Knots

When making a piece with willow, sometimes you have to be able to tie together rods or twigs. A sustainable and beautiful way to keep them together is to make a knot from a pliant willow twig. Use a thin 80 cm–100 cm long willow twig.

JAPANESE EYE

1 Fold the twig 90 degrees, about 10 cm from the thick end and place it perpendicular to the rods that are to be linked together. Wrap the twig around the willow rods, and loop the twig over its end that is sticking out. Bend the twig back around the willow rods, underneath the initial ring.

2 The thick end of the twig forms the "eye center," and the knot is made around it. Continue to tie the twig's end in from different directions. When it loops around the eye, the twig should be tied alternating one time from the bottom up and one time from the top down.

3 Place every loop edge to edge in order to tie a flat and pretty eye. Keep tying until you have used the entire twig.

4 Secure the narrow end of the twig by inserting it into the knot and pulling it through to the other side. Use an awl if it's difficult to get the end through the knot. Finally, trim the ends that stick out from the knot.

CROSS KNOT

1 Use a thin 80 cm long willow twig. Start with the thick end of the wrapping twig. Wrap the twig around the rods that are to be tied together and wrap the twig diagonally, up over its own end.

2 Continue to bring the wrapping twig down along the rods and up on the other side. Place the twig diagonally across the rods again but in the opposite direction so that it runs parallel to the twig's thick end.

3 Continue wrapping the twig around the rods, alternating upward and downward, so that a diagonal grid forms on the front. Place every wrap edge to edge so the knot is flat and smooth. Continue until you reach the end of the twig.

4 Secure the narrow end by sticking it into the knot and pulling it out the opposite side. If the knot is tied tightly, you may need to use an awl. Finally, trim any ends that are sticking out from the knot.

COILED KNOT

1. Fold the thick end of the twig against the rods that are to be tied together.
2. Wrap the twig tightly around the rods and over its own end. For a small knot, 3–4 wraps are enough. If you would like a wider knot, continue to wrap until you reach the end of the twig.
3. Finish by inserting the loose end of the wrapping twig between the rods and the tie. Pull it tight and trim the end. Use an awl to open up a hole for the twig if it is too tight.

TWISTED WILLOW TREE

Willow is a really fun material to work with. Willow twigs are so flexible that they can be shaped in the most astonishing ways. Fresh willow branches easily build roots and grow very fast. If you plant a willow twig in the ground and water it properly, it will soon become a new willow tree. Making a small willow tree with a twisted stem is simple. The stem will start sprouting leaves and a little crown will take shape after only a few weeks.

MATERIALS

- 9 twigs of equal thickness, 2–2.5 m in length
- Cord

TOOLS

- Pruning shears
- Scissors

Simple variations

A simple braid of three rods.

A simple braid and a simple twist of three thin twigs.

A braid of nine thin twigs.

Salix

STEP BY STEP

Select long, fresh willow twigs; they should have about the same thickness. The thicker the twigs are, the harder it will be to shape the stem. Remember that the twigs need plenty of water before they can be planted. Trim the sprouts at the top so that they branch out and the crown becomes denser.

1 Tie the thick ends of 3 twigs together. Place the knot about 7 cm from the bottom. Make three bundles.

2 Pick up one bundle and hold the thick ends of the twigs in your right hand. Separate the twigs with the left hand and let the thinner ends run freely between your fingers. Then twist the twigs with your right hand.

3 Tie the twigs 20–30 cm from the top. Repeat with the other two bundles.

4 Tie the three twisted bundles together at the thick ends.

5 Twist the three bundles just like you did with each separate one, and finish by tying the twisted stem together 20–30 cm from the top.

6 With pruning shears, cut about 5 cm off the root end of each willow twig so they get a fresh cut.

7 Immediately put the twisted stem into a bucket of water. Let the twigs stand for approximately 3–5 days to store plenty of water.

8 Plant the stem in the ground or in a pot, as deep as it was in the water. Water it plentifully and often. Willow trees love water and need a lot of it to grow. Preferably, water the willow enough that there will be water on the pot's tray at all times.

9 Trim the top ends so only 10–20 cm remains above the knot.

10 Leaves will start to grow after only a few weeks. Remove the shoots regularly from the stem and let the topmost shoots form the tree's crown.

CHAPTER No 9

CASTING CONCRETE

A Moldable Favorite

Concrete can easily be understood as cold and hard, but it's actually a fantastic material to work with. With simple plastic molds, you can cast pretty and durable items. The smoother the walls of the molds are, the finer the surface of the concrete will be. In this chapter, you will find both small and easy projects and more demanding ones. The garden frog, the paperweights, and the conical lanterns can all be made quickly and without hassle. The personalized discs and concrete bench take a lot more concrete and will demand more work.

In the midst of the great city of Rome, there stands the 2,000-year-old Pantheon with its 45 meter wide concrete dome roof that can only be glimpsed from the outside. The inside is equally dazzling; the oculus, the large hole at the top of the dome has an incredible diameter of 9 meters.

Plastic and silicone make good molds. The concrete is easily removed from their edges. Custom molds can be built from wood and particle board.

I n today's larger edifices, concrete is often one of the main building materials. Concrete's primary properties are resistance and strength. Since concrete is moldable, it is useful in bridge and tunnel construction.

Hard but Smooth

Concrete is made from an aggregate material and cement that are mixed with water. Aggregate material contains different fractions of stone, gravel, or sand, depending on how the concrete is to be used. Cement consists mainly of heated ground limestone and clay. Today's cement, Portland cement, is based on an English patent from 1824.

Concrete has compressive strength. However, it doesn't have high tensile strength. Therefore, rebars are cast into the concrete. Sometimes fibers are mixed in the pulp to increase the tensile strength.

There are a variety of concrete mixtures. I use three of them in this book: fine concrete, coarse concrete, and expanding concrete. As the name suggests, the fine concrete contains finer fractions of sand compared with coarse concrete. Generally, fine concrete is used for layers 2–10 cm thick, coarse concrete is used for 5 cm layers or thicker, and expanding concrete is used for creating an extremely neat finish and durable corners.

Many Great Molds

In order to cast concrete objects, molds are required. Large molds built from wood and plywood or form plywood (as it's also called) have a coated surface that is water-resistant, so they're easy to remove from the concrete. The mold is important, as it is what creates the exterior of the concrete object. Smaller objects can be molded in plastic jars and cardboard tubes, to provide a few examples.

Should You Mix The Concrete Yourself?

If you need large amounts of concrete, you can buy it ready mixed and have it delivered to the site directly in a concrete mixer. Otherwise you can buy cement and ballast separately and mix it yourself. The easiest way, but a little more expensive, is to buy premixed dry concrete in bags of 15–20 kg. This is what I did to make the projects in this chapter. All you need to do is add the water (the mixing ratio is described on the packaging). After a while, you'll get a feel for how much water is needed.

SAFETY

Mixing and managing large amounts of concrete is heavy work. It's better to make multiple batches than to load too much concrete in your bucket; this way, the burden on your shoulders and joints is lessened.

• Concrete is corrosive and harmful to the airways, so always use respiratory protection when handling dry concrete.

• Wear safety goggles to protect against splashes of concrete when mixing.

• Since concrete dries out the skin, it's best to use gloves when working. If you need to work with your hands in the ready-mixed concrete, it's vital that you wear heavy gloves.

A concrete mixer attached to an electric screwdriver facilitates the mixing.

The consistency of premixed concrete is about as thick as porridge.

A Brief History

About 2,500 years ago, a concrete-like material was used in the Roman Empire. The Romans used this ancient concrete to make buildings, aqueducts, and amphitheaters. Many of these mighty buildings still remain to be seen. But after the fall of the Roman Empire, concrete-making technology was forgotten. It was rediscovered in the 15th century, but it was only at the end of the 18th century that the technology was employed again.

Patterned ceiling panels and cornices in foam are perfect for creating beautiful patterns in the concrete.

Small amounts of concrete can be mixed by hand using a trowel and a small plastic bucket. Small amounts of concrete, such as a half a bag, can be mixed in a bucket with a mixing paddle. A mixing paddle is a type of attachment for a drill or electric screwdriver.

To mix greater amounts of concrete, you'll need a concrete mixer. The machine will do the leg work but you'll still have to lift the heavy bags of concrete.

Remove Any Air Bubbles

When the concrete is mixed and has been placed in the mold, it needs to be compressed. The goal is to fill the mold completely with the concrete and to remove any air bubbles. This can be done by tapping the mold with a rubber mallet or with a trowel. The denser the concrete, the better the quality.

Porous concrete can absorb moisture, and if the pores get filled with water, the concrete can freeze and burst.

Curing the Concrete

Within hours the concrete mass will harden thanks to the chemical reaction that occurs when cement is mixed with water. Heat is produced and this process is called "curing." If you spray water on the concrete during the curing process, or if you cover it with plastic, the evaporation will be reduced. This lengthens the time it takes for the concrete to cure, and the concrete becomes stronger.

Recycling

Some wooden molds are disposable. You just tear them apart and throw them out when the concrete has finished curing. Plastic, silicone, and rubber molds or those that are constructed with particle board can be reused many times if you clean them carefully after casting. Remove any concrete residue from the mold. Then wash it with warm soapy water, rinse with clean water, and wipe dry.

Purchasing

In most home improvement stores you can find the concrete and the material to make custom molds as shown in the book. Plastic and silicone molds are available in most hobby shops. It's also a great idea to reuse plastic food packaging. These tend to be smooth and fine, and are available in a wide variety of shapes and sizes.

FROG

I like little surprises in the garden. These can be small statues in gleaming white marble that pop out from behind the hedges, or even moss-covered rocks that evoke images of elves and trolls. Something else that can trigger my thoughts are stones of different stratifications. How and when was that bright line formed in the stone, and what made half of the stone red and the other half black? Insects and frogs belong to the garden, and a small frog is simple to make in concrete. My concrete frog looks out from a large carpet of thyme.

MATERIALS

- 1 plastic mold
- Vegetable oil
- 600 ml mixed expanding concrete
- Murphy Oil Soap, or other natural wood cleaner

TOOLS

- Rags
- Small bucket
- Trowel

Water-repellent Surface

To get a smooth and water-resistant surface you can treat the concrete with natural wood cleaner and water. It makes it easy to clean it when it becomes soiled. Mix Murphy's oil soap, or other natural wood cleaner, with water according to package directions. Dab the object with the soap water and let the liquid be absorbed by the concrete. Wait for 5 minutes. Repeat 3–4 times or until the concrete is saturated. Finish by polishing the concrete surface with a soft lint-free cloth to make the surface shiny.

Thymus

STEP BY STEP

The mold is recyclable, so you can make several frogs. Give one to a friend or put them in surprising places in the garden. The mold can be purchased at the craft store.

1 Dampen the cloth with vegetable oil and grease the walls of the mold. They should be only slightly moist. Wipe off any excess oil that puddles at the bottom of the mold.

2 Support the sides of the frog shape so the frog hangs freely in the air. Check that the form hangs straight. Mix the concrete according to the instructions on the package. Pour the concrete into the mold so that it's halfway full. Tap the mold gently with the trowel so the air bubbles rise from the concrete.

3 Pour some more concrete to fill the mold completely. Flatten the concrete with the trowel. Make sure there is enough concrete that the frog's toes are properly filled in.

4 Tap the mold again with the trowel to remove any air bubbles. Allow the concrete to set for 3–4 days.

5 Gently remove the frog by tipping the mold over. Hold one hand over the mold to catch the frog. You may have to wiggle the mold back and forth to release the frog.

6 If the frog is going to be placed outdoors it's useful to treat it with Murphy's oil soap. (see previous page). Wash the mold in warm, soapy water.

Fragrant Flower Bed

The Greek word *thyein* means "smell," and this is just what thyme, *Thymus*, does. Thyme is a low, creeping dwarf shrub that loves sunny, dry, and calcareous soils. The lowest varieties form dense beds that spread a wonderful aroma when you touch them. A thriving plant can soon grow to cover many square feet. It is not as durable as a lawn but it can handle a couple of footsteps without a problem.

Often thyme has tiny green, gray, or yellow leaves. Although the flowers are small, there are so many that the bed is completely covered with white, pink, or violet flowers.

In Sweden there are two domestic species: wild thyme and large thyme. The plant is mentioned in pharmaceutical texts as early as the 15th century. Today, thyme is mainly used as a spice. It has a rich aroma and is strongly associated with pea soup. The taste is also good in meat stews and tomato and fish soups.

NAPKIN WEIGHTS

The afternoon's sea breeze provides a lovely coolness in the summer heat. But if the table is set, the napkins will fly away. This, however, can be remedied with small weights, which you can easily make from concrete. The hard, heavy concrete is a nice contrast to the soft and warm heart shape I've chosen to mold. If you make the napkin weights with expanding concrete and a smooth mold, the surface will be velvety soft. It's reminiscent of the stones that float up on the beach, which I loved to caress on my cheek as a child. Cute pot feet can be cast in the same way as ice in an ice cube tray. These can be found on page 49.

MATERIALS

To make two hearts:
• 1 plastic mold
• Vegetable oil
• 250 ml mixed expanding concrete

TOOLS

• Brush or cloth
• Small bucket
• Trowel

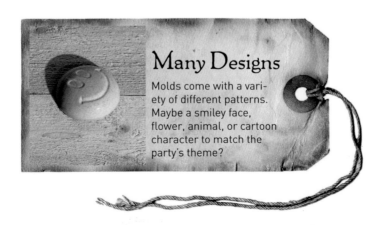

Many Designs

Molds come with a variety of different patterns. Maybe a smiley face, flower, animal, or cartoon character to match the party's theme?

STEP BY STEP

Plastic molds can be found in craft stores.
Soap, plaster, and concrete molds work well.

1 Pour a few drops of vegetable oil in the mold. Use a brush or a cloth to spread the oil around the mold. Wipe off any excess.

2 Mix the concrete in a small bucket according to the package instructions. Fill the mold with concrete. Gently tap the trowel against the mold to remove the air bubbles. Flatten the concrete surface with the trowel.

3 Place the mold on a flat surface and allow the concrete to cure for 2–3 days.

4 Tilt the pan upside down and catch each concrete heart as it releases from the mold. Wash the mold in warm, soapy water so it can be reused.

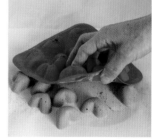

Pot Feet

If you stand outdoor pots on plates, they risk drowning in the rain. But if the pots stand directly on the ground, ants will invade. Pot feet made of concrete keep the ants away and let excess water drain. Use an ice cube mold made of silicone rubber. Place the dish on a flat surface and fill it with about 150 ml fine concrete or expandable concrete. Even the surface with the trowel and let the concrete cure for two days. Remove the concrete hearts and wash the mold in lukewarm soapy water.

DECORATIVE FLOWERPOT BASE

Large flowerpot bases are surprisingly expensive to buy in anything other than plastic. Terracotta bases are fine for terracotta pots, but they don't look as nice with concrete, stone, and ceramic pots. If you have an old silver-plated platter that you don't mind getting dirty, you can use that to make a beautiful concrete base. All metal plates work, but they should have a decorative edge. The metal plate's ornate border will be transferred to the concrete, and the flowerpot base may get a soft, smooth feel.

MATERIALS

Makes a 30 cm-diameter concrete tray.
- Silver-plated or steel tray with a beautiful border
- Vegetable oil
- 700 ml expanding concrete, mixed
- Plastic gloves
- Murphy Oil Soap, or other natural wood cleaner
- 4 self-adhesive felt pads or silicone pads

TOOLS

- Rags
- Small bucket
- Trowel

PLANTS

- Hortensia, *Hydrangea macrophylla* (1 pc)

Pretty for Fruits and Vegetables

This subtle ash gray concrete tray makes a lovely fruit and vegetable dish. Treat the surface with soap (see the tips on page 45) to make it easier to clean the plate.

Hydrangea macrophylla

STEP BY STEP

If you don't have a dish at home that you want to use, try a thrift shop. You can usually find plates with beautiful edges in silver or steel here.

1 Coat the back of the plate with a fine layer of vegetable oil. The entire surface should be covered. Remove any excess from the shaped edges. Put the silver platter face down on a flat surface.

2 Mix the concrete according to the directions on the package. Don't make the mix too thin. The consistency should be similar to modeling clay. Wear plastic gloves and use your hands to stretch the concrete over the back of the platter.

3 Cover the bottom of the plate with an even layer of smooth concrete. Press the concrete on the edges of the platter so the folded rim fills with concrete. Let the concrete cure for 3–4 days.

4 Gently remove the platter. Wash it with soapy water so it can be reused.

5 Finish the concrete base with Murphy's oil soap so the surface becomes water repellent (see page 45).

6 Turn the base upside down. Affix protective pads to the bottom so it doesn't scratch any delicate surface.

Genus *Hydrangea*

Hydrangeas are available as both indoor and outdoor plants. They need moisture-retaining soil; water moderately, keeping the soil moist but not soggy, and avoid letting the hydrangeas sit in water. If the hydrangeas dry out, the buds may fall off. Hydrangea blossoms in white, blue, pink, or red, and flower clusters may be several inches in size. In acidic soil, a pink hydrangea can change color and turn blue. In the same way, blue hydrangeas can turn pink if the pH in the soil is too high. It's important to keep the soil acidic if you want to keep the blue color.

Hydrangeas first came from Japan. In their natural environment, they can grow several feet tall. In Madeira and the Azores, there are great clusters of hydrangeas because the cool, humid climate is perfect for them. Along roadsides and pastures, hydrangea hedges can stretch for miles.

Hydrangea arborescens "Annabelle"

Climbing Hortensia, *Hydrangea anomala* ssp. *petiolaris*

Hortensia, *Hydrangea macrophylla*

Pinky winky, *Hydrangea paniculata*

GARDEN PARTY VASE

Birthday parties, graduation celebrations, or a baptism out in the garden on a hot and sunny summer will become a memory for life. The middle of the green outdoors is probably the best party location one can find. You can hear the birds chirping and be caressed by the warm winds. A lovely bouquet of flowers on the table adds an extra bit of welcome. To make sure the wind doesn't blow it over, you can put the bouquet in a concrete vase.

MATERIALS

- Double-sided carpet tape
- 1 plastic flower pot (10 cm in diameter, 18 cm high)
- Duct tape
- Vegetable oil
- 2 liters of mixed fine concrete
- 1 drinking glass (6–7 cm in diameter, 15 cm high)
- Masking tape

TOOLS

- Scissors
- Cloth
- Small bucket
- Trowel
- Hammer or rubber mallet
- Wire cutters

PLANTS

Seven kinds of wild flowers.

- Daisy, *Leucanthemum vulgare*
- Mayflower, *Geranium sylvaticum*
- Water Avens, *Geum rivale*
- Buttercup, *Ranunculus acris*
- Northern Bedstraw, *Galium boreale*
- Red clover, *Trifolium pratense*
- Timothy, *Phleum pratense*

STEP BY STEP

The tall and narrow plastic pots that climbers are often planted in make ideal molds. By taping a leaf to the inside of the pot, the vase will get a leaf-pattern decoration. Choose a leaf that has prominent veins so the cast is clear. I used rhododendron leaves. Including a drinking glass in the vase makes cleaning easy.

1 Attach two rhododendron leaves with their smooth topsides against a piece of double-sided tape. The rear veins should face upward.

2 Cut the leaves and carefully remove the protective film from the tape.

3 Tape the leaves to the inside of the plastic pot. Put them on opposite sides of the pot.

4 Cover all the holes in the bottom of the pot with duct tape. It's better to cover them from the inside, but if it's too difficult to reach, cover them from the outside of the pot.

5 Pour a bit of vegetable oil on a cloth and grease the inside of the pot.

6 Mix the concrete according to the directions on the package. Pour some concrete into the bottom of the pot. Fill the drinking glass with gravel and place it in the middle of the pot on top of the concrete.

7 Fill the pot up with concrete—around the glass—and smooth out the surface with a trowel. Tap the mold with a hammer or rubber mallet to remove any air bubbles.

8 Put masking tape over the pot so the glass is held in place and doesn't move as the concrete cures. Let the concrete cure for 3–4 days.

9 Pour the gravel from the glass. Turn the vase upside down and remove the plastic pot. You may have to cut it with scissors and pull it apart.

10 The concrete vase is ready for a lovely bouquet.

HERB POTS

Fresh herbs bring both delightful aromas and flavors to your kitchen and your cooking. Some herbs are easy to grow and will thrive in the vegetable garden. Parsley and chives can be grown outside well into the fall. Others require a lot of warmth and special conditions for overwintering. But today we don't need to go without fresh herbs—even during the winter. You can buy many varieties of herb plants year round at the grocery store. Whether you prepare dinner in your kitchen or barbecue on the patio in the summer heat, it's practical and stylish to place the little herb plant in a sturdy concrete pot. You can even cast several pieces so you'll have a pot for all your favorite herbs. On page 59, there's a guide for crafting pots for succulents in a similar manner.

MATERIALS

Makes one herb pot.

- 1 plastic pot for outer shape (500 ml)
- 1 plastic pot for inner shape (200 ml)
- 300 ml expanding concrete, mixed
- Wet sand paper, 80 grit

TOOLS

- Small bucket
- Trowel
- Wire cutters

Petroselinum crispum

STEP BY STEP

Many grocery store items come in plastic containers, and these make great molds. Where I live, the 200 ml containers of sour cream are the perfect size for fresh herb plants. A 500 ml container can be used as an outer mold to make a pot of moderate thickness.

1 Wash the plastic packaging and check that there will be at least 5 mm of space between the containers when they are stacked.

2 With a trowel, mix the water and the concrete in a small bucket according to the instructions on the packaging. Pour concrete in the bottom of the larger plastic container.

3 Fill the smaller container with gravel and place it inside the large container. The small container's top rim should be raised slightly above that of the larger container. Adjust the height by either topping with some more concrete or by pressing the small container deeper into the concrete.

4 With a trowel, lay concrete in the gap between the containers. Let the concrete stand and cure for 3–4 days. When the concrete has cured completely, pour out the gravel.

5 Cut the rims on both containers as shown above. Pull the tabs away and remove the pot.

6 Moisten the concrete pot and use sandpaper to grind away any irregularities. Clean the dust from the surface with water. The pot is now ready to be filled with fresh herbs.

Label the Herb Pots

In my home country of Sweden, herb plants often come with lovely labels. Sometimes these labels include information about which dishes the herbs can be used in. Cut these labels from the packaging and tape them to the concrete pots to give a decorative and informative embellishment.

Echeveria, *Echeveria* "Miranda"

Succulents either store water in their thick and fleshy leaves or in their stems. Those with fleshy leaves are called "fat leaf" plants, and those that store water in the stem are called "stem succulents."

Shape, appearance, and size can vary significantly between different species. Succulents thrive in well-drained soil. If they get too wet, then they rot. Succulents grow quite slowly but they are durable and persistent.

The succulents that grow as indoor plants won't say no to nutrients during the summer. They also enjoy being moved to a sunny and warm spot in the garden. However, they rest in the winter, when they like to be cool and completely dry.

Paradise Tree, *Crassula ovata*

Haworthia, *Haworthia attenuata*, "Zebra Plant"

Flaming Katy, *Kalanchoe*

Succulent Pot

Succulents do very well in concrete pots. Succulents are drought-tolerant and aren't choosy about soil. A succulent pot is made the same way as an herb pot; the only difference is that it needs proper drainage holes in the bottom. A salad bowl and a plastic container that holds 800 ml make good molds. With a knife, cut two wine corks in half and tape three cork halves to the bottom of the bowl. Mix the concrete (approx. 900 ml) and pour enough concrete into the bowl to align with the tops of the corks. Brush the outside of the plastic container with cooking oil. Fill the container with gravel and place it on top of the corks. Fill the bowl with concrete. Allow the concrete to cure for 3–4 days. Remove the mold and poke the corks from the bottom of the concrete pot. Now the drainage holes should be exposed. Place some potsherds (broken pieces of ceramic material) over the drainage holes to allow drainage without losing any soil. Plant the succulent in the pot.

CONICAL VOTIVE

Pyramids, cones, and spheres are exciting geo-
metrical forms. Sometimes, palace gardens trim
their yews into pyramids. Boxwood is often
trimmed into spheres and cones, but these are
also two of the tree's naturally occurring shapes.
You can fit the beautiful cone shape into your
garden with these small concrete votives. These
are easy to make and easy to set up. Just stick
the tip of the cone down into the ground (or set
it in a pot) where you'd like some pleasant light
for when dusk falls. You can also make square
candle holders for the table, and these instructions are on the next page.

MATERIALS

Makes one votive.
- 1 plastic champagne flute, approx. 120 ml
- 1 plastic salad dressing cup, 60 ml (62 x 30 mm)
- 150 ml expanding concrete, mixed
- Masking tape
- Wet sand paper, 80–120 grit

TOOLS

- Small bucket
- Trowel
- Wooden stick
- Needle-nose pliers

Floating Votives

Small votives can be effective sources
of light against the winter darkness.
You can "float" the votives below the
tree branches by placing them in simple iron holders. For a description of
how to make the holders, see page 181.

Buxus

STEP BY STEP

For the inner shape of the conical lantern, I use plastic salad dressing cups (the kind you get when you buy a salad or other fast food). The size is perfect for a standard tea light.

1 Mix the concrete according to the instructions on the packaging. Fill the champagne flute with concrete until it is about 1 cm below the rim. Remove the air bubbles by pumping a wooden stick up and down in the concrete.

2 Press the salad dressing cup down into the concrete. Make sure it's centered. Fill the cup with gravel so it doesn't move.

3 Secure the cup to the champagne flute with masking tape. Ensure that the cup is centered in the flute. Place the flute on a flat surface and let the concrete cure for 2–3 days.

4 Remove the tape and pour out the stones. Remove the plastic cup from the concrete. Hold the concrete cone and flip the champagne flute back and forth. It will usually loosen and can then be reused.

5 If the champagne flute doesn't detach from the concrete, you'll need tongs to remove the plastic piece by piece.

6 Wet the concrete and sand down the top edge with wet sandpaper. Rinse off any dust with water. Place a tea light in the candleholder and insert the conical votive straight into the ground.

Square Candleholders

This candleholder is made in the same manner as the conical votives, but instead use a 210 ml (72 x 72 x 72 mm) plastic dessert cup instead of a champagne flute. Fill the pastry cup with concrete; leave about 0.5 cm from the rim. Press a salad dressing cup filled with gravel into the concrete and make sure it is centered. Let the concrete cure. Remove the molds and polish the top with wet sandpaper. Put adhesive pads on the bottom of the candleholder so it doesn't scratch whatever surface you put it on.

UNIQUE CONCRETE SLABS

Casting your own concrete slabs is inexpensive and fun. You can use mosaic tiles and other fun little odds and ends as decorative details on the slabs. You can create a walkway by putting the ornate slabs down on the lawn as stepping-stones. If you make your slabs a standard size, you can easily combine your home-made slabs with the store-bought variety. With a few personalized slabs, a large area can immediately become exciting and comfy. On page 133 you will find a description of a walkway I made using these slabs.

MATERIALS

Makes one 4-slab mold.

- 1 piece formwork
  (12 x 786 x 1086 mm)
- 3.1 m planed wood stud (25
  x 50 mm)
- 20 wood screws
  (4 x 30 mm)

Makes four concrete slabs.

- Plywood pieces (different
  sizes and thicknesses)
- Spray glue
- Vaseline or cooking oil
- 50 kg concrete
- 4 pieces chicken wire
  (30 x 30 cm)
- Decorative stones and other
  beautiful details
- 1 piece of protective plastic
  film (80 x 80 cm)
- Tile adhesive primer
- Tile adhesive for outdoor
  use
- Tile grout for outdoor use

TOOLS

- Saw
- Ruler
- Drill driver
- Drill bit (3 mm)
- Spirit level
- Soft rags
- Concrete mixing paddle or
  stirrers
- Bucket
- Trowel
- Hammer
- Crowbar
- Brush or roller
- Notched trowel
- Joint filler
- Sponge

STEP BY STEP
[Building the mold]

I have chosen to make the slabs 5 x 35 x 35 cm in size. This is the size of the standard slabs that can be bought at home improvement stores. This 4-slab mold is reusable if you clean it after each casting.

1 Cut the plywood to 78.6 x 78.6 cm. This will form the base of the mold.

2 Cut the planed wood stud into two pieces, each 73.6 cm long and two pieces that are 78.6 cm long. Pre-drill the holes for the screws and screw the wood stud pieces along the edge of the underside of the base. The inside dimensions of the mold should be 73.6 x 73.6 cm.

3 Cut six pieces of plywood to be 5 cm wide; these will be the mold's removable dividers. Cut four of the plywood pieces to be 73.6 cm long and two pieces to be 71.2 cm. Cut the joints to be half of the plywood piece's width, as illustrated in the design sketch. Each joint is 12 mm so that the pieces fit tightly.

4 Assemble the mold. Mark the assembled pieces of the frame so you will have an easier time putting the mold together next time.

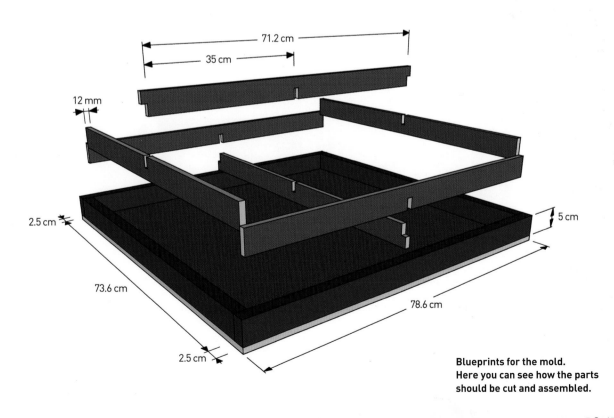

**Blueprints for the mold.
Here you can see how the parts should be cut and assembled.**

STEP BY STEP
[Casting concrete slabs]

Place the mold on a stable surface and use a spirit level to confirm that it lies flat. To make room for any inset decorations, glue solid plywood boards to the bottom of the mold. This will cause recesses to form in the finished slab; mosaic pieces can be inserted in these recesses.

1 Adjust the plywood boards to the size and thickness of the intended decoration. Decorations can also be cast directly into the concrete. Glue the decorations or the boards onto the bottom of the mold. Here seven metal nuts have been glued into the shape of a flower.

2 Brush the sides of the mold with vegetable oil so it doesn't stick to the concrete. Fill the mold halfway with concrete. Reinforce with wire mesh and fill the rest of the mold.

3 Smooth the concrete with a trowel. Tap the mold with a hammer to remove any air bubbles. Cover with plastic and let the concrete cure for 3–4 days.

4 Remove the mold's partitions and remove the slabs. Screw some screws into the plywood boards and use a crowbar to pry them up. Be careful not to damage the concrete slab.

5 Apply a primer to the decorative recess. The primer will improve the stickiness of the tile adhesive on the concrete.

6 Wait for the primer to dry; it will shift slightly in color when dry. This only takes about 10 minutes. Apply tile adhesive to the primed recess. Use a notched trowel to spread the adhesive to the proper thickness.

7 Place decorative stones or tile on the adhesive layer. Press lightly to secure them. Here, I used some small tiles that were left over from when we redid the bathroom.

8 After at least two days (when the adhesive has set properly) add the tile joint compound to the gaps between the ceramic tiles. Work the tile joint compound into the gaps by smoothing the grout diagonally across the slabs with a joint filler tool. Wait 10 minutes.

9 Wipe off any excess grout with a wet sponge. Rinse the sponge in clean water. Wipe the tiles several times until all excess grout is removed.

10 Polish away the last of the grout with a soft cloth. The concrete slab is now ready to use.

Examples of Finished Slabs

Some of these slabs have been used in the unique walkway (see page 133).

Recessed dark gray tiles.

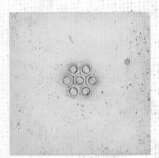

Large metal nuts form a floral pattern in the center of the slab.

Flat stones on mesh are recessed into the concrete slab.

Three round coins fixed in the tile adhesive.

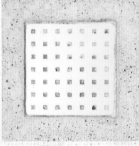

A recessed decorative plate in aluminum.

Recessed dark gray ceramic strips.

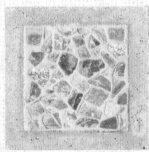

An iron heart in the middle of the slab.

Recessed plastic letters with a framework of mosaic pieces.

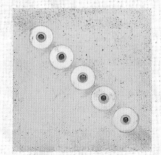

Washers recessed into the concrete and glass beads mounted with tile adhesive.

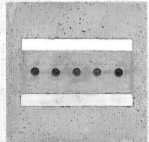

Recessed aluminum strips and five glass beads fixed with tile adhesive.

Mosaic pieces in white, blue, and black form a symmetrical pattern.

An Alfa Romeo hood ornament mounted with tile adhesive.

SLAB WITH A LACY EDGE

In the house, we adorn tables with sheer lace cloths, and place vases on elegant pedestals. These are often highly decorative; nineteenth century majolica pedestals, for example, have leaf ornamentation and gilt decoration. This concrete slab isn't as showy as that, but the concrete's natural ash color and smooth texture make a beautiful base for a pot or vase. With a lace-like pattern along the edge, the slab will takes on a softer appearance, reminiscent of a lace doily. The slab can be a decorative piece when placed directly on the ground, but it's also ready for use as a pedestal top. Instructions for the stand are given on page 209.

Instructions for the stand are given on page 209.

MATERIALS

For the mold
- 1 piece of formwork (12 x 470 x 470 mm)
- 1.7 m wood stud (45 x 45 mm)
- 12 wood screws (4 x 30 mm)

Makes one small slab (29 x 29 cm).
- 1.4 m wood stud (45 x 45 mm)
- 1.2 m Styrofoam decorative panel (31 x 31 mm)
- Vegetable oil
- 4.5 liter store-bought, bagged concrete
- 1 sheet of chicken wire (22 x 22 cm)
- 1 piece of plywood (47 x 47 cm)
- 20 cm round steel rod (8 mm)
- Electrical tape

TOOLS

- Ruler
- Saw
- Drill driver
- Drill bit (3 mm and 9 mm)
- Hacksaw
- Miter box
- Spirit level
- Cloth
- Bucket
- Trowel
- Concrete mixing paddle
- Shears
- Hammer
- Scissors
- Bolt cutter

STEP BY STEP

Start with the mold. The one I chose has solid edges; however, you can use loose spacers to easily adapt the mold to form panels of different dimensions. Loose spacers also allow the concrete to release easily from the mold. The slab can be made in two sizes. Here's the description for the smaller slab, which is meant to rest on a pedestal stand. If you don't want it for a pedestal, you can skip steps 11–15.

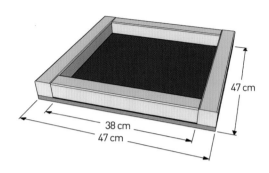

Cut the stud for the mold into four pieces: two that are 47 cm long and two that are 38 cm long. Place the stud pieces onto the formwork according to the above design. Pre-drill holes for screws and screw the mold together from the underside of the formwork.

1 Cut two of the 45 x 45 mm thick frame pieces to be 38 cm long and the other two pieces to be 29 cm in length. Align the pieces with the frame's inner edge.

2 Cut two pieces of the styrofoam decorative panel to be 29 cm long. Place the two pieces inside the mold, on opposite sides.

3 Take a new styrofoam panel and cut both ends at a 45° angle. It will be easier if you use a miter box. Make sure the panel is facing the right direction. Measure how long the panel should be and cut the edge at a 45° angle. Cut another foam strip in the same way.

4 Place the mitered styrofoam panels on top of the inner frame pieces. Check that the miters (the joints) are tight together and are not gaping. This is to prevent any concrete from spilling through the gaps.

5 Place the mold on a flat surface. Use a spirit level to confirm that it lies flat.

6 Grease the foam strips and the inside of the mold with the vegetable oil. Remove any excess oil.

7 Mix the concrete according to the instructions on the bag. Fill the mold halfway with concrete.

8 Push the chicken wire down firmly into the concrete. By reinforcing the slab with the chicken wire, the slab will be stronger and will last longer.

[70]   CASTING CONCRETE

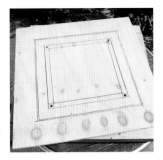

9 Fill the rest of the frame with concrete and smooth the surface with a trowel.

10 Gently tap the frame with a hammer to remove any air bubbles from the wet concrete.

11 Draw the concrete slab's dimensions (29 x 29 cm) in the center of the 47 x 47 cm plywood sheet. Also, draw the outer edge dimensions (22 x 22 cm) for the top of the pedestal chassis. The width of the chassis' top frame should be 15 mm. Drill a hole 9 mm in size in the middle of the marks that delineate the chassis's corners.

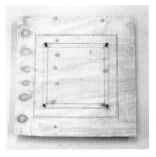

12 Cut the round steel rod into four pieces that are 5 cm in length. Wrap about one half of each rod in electrical tape to stop the bars from falling through the holes at the corners of the frame.

13 Check that the rods fit into the drilled holes.

14 Place the plywood sheet with the rods (tape side up) on top of the concrete-filled frame. The rods should be pressed into the wet concrete. Make sure the plywood sheet is centered on the frame. Let the concrete cure for 3–4 days.

15 Remove the electrical tape from the rods and gently remove the plywood sheet.

16 Once the concrete is completely cured, gently flip the frame upside down and detach the slab.

17 Remove the styrofoam panels from the concrete. The slab is now complete. If you want to make the surface water-repellent, treat it with soapy water (see tip p. 45). Instructions for a large slab are available in the sidebar.

Large Slab with a Lace Border

The mold can also be used to make a large slab with the dimensions of 33 x 33 cm. Cut the frame open and use a spacer in the frame. Prepare the slab in the same way you would prepare the smaller slab, but remember that the outer dimensions for the chassis' top frame should be 26 x 26 cm.

MATERIALS

Materials for a large slab (33 x 33 cm).

- 1.5 m wood stud (25 x 45 mm)
- 1.4 m decorative Styrofoam panel (31 x 31 mm), e.g. Decosa 'Martine'
- Vegetable oil
- 5.5 liter mixed concrete
- 1 sheet of chicken wire (26 x 26 cm)
- 1 sheet of plywood (47 x 47 cm)
- 20 cm round steel rod (8 mm)
- Electrical tape

CONCRETE BENCH

A garden needs small nooks where you can go to relax. You can easily move a chair when you want to follow the sun's rays, but a concrete bench isn't something that can be shifted around at a whim. Wood, concrete, and iron make an exciting combination. This bench brings steadiness and stability to the garden. Plus, it becomes more rustically beautiful with the passage of time; the iron will start to rust and the wood becomes weathered and gray.

An Alternative

Getting a hold of a solid wooden board that is 10 cm thick and 38.5 cm wide may be tricky. One alternative is to build the bench top in commercially available dimensions. Try using planed wood with the dimensions of 45 x 95 cm and 45 x 145 cm.

MATERIALS

FOR THE MOLD

- 1 form plywood board (12 x 600 x 1300 mm)
- Masking tape
- 20 wood screws (4 x 30 mm)
- 40 cm pvc pipe (16 mm)

FOR THE BENCH AND THE PAVING STONE BASE

- 100 kg concrete
- 5 m rebar (8 mm)
- 1 piece of protective plastic film (1 x 1 m)
- 1 iron pipe of 106 cm (2.6 x 21.3 mm)
- 2 threaded rods of 1 m (10 mm)
- 2 splice nuts M10
- 4 square washers M10 (30 x 30 mm)
- 2 dome nuts M10
- 1 wooden plank (100 x 385 x 1200 mm)
- 350 liter of gravel (⁹⁄₁₆)
- 3 m² ground cloth
- 1.5 m² Öland stone
- 4.8 m wooden planks for frame
- 4 brackets
- 8 wood screws (4 x 30 mm)
- Paving sand

TOOLS

- Ruler and spirit level
- Circular saw or jigsaw
- Drill driver
- Drill bit (3 mm and 16 mm)
- Clamps
- Hacksaw and bolt cutter
- Concrete mixer
- Bucket and trowel
- Rubber mallet
- Marking sticks
- Trowel and broom
- Soil compactor
- Angle grinder

STEP BY STEP
[Building the mold]

The bench consists of two concrete sidepieces. You can simply make one mold and cast one sidepiece at a time. When finished, they will weigh almost 50 kg, so it's to your advantage to cast them on site. A solid wooden plank for the seat can be difficult to come by in a traditional lumberyard. Sometimes the joinery and timber stores can order custom pieces straight from the sawmill. You can also build the seat following the tip on the previous page.

1 Measure and mark all parts of the mold on the plywood board. Use the dimensions from the spec drawing of the bench's side pieces (see below to the right).

2 Cut out the pieces with a circular saw or jigsaw.

3 Screw together a long side and a short side. Always pre-drill the holes for the screws so the wood does not split.

4 Assemble the small pieces that will form the recess for the bench seat. Use the clamps to hold the parts together during assembly. Screw the pieces to the long side of the mold.

5 The recess for the seat is ready.

6 Attach the mold's bottom and the second long side.

7 Attach the mold's second short side.

8 Drill a hole 16 mm wide in the middle of one of the long sides (see the spec drawing).

9 Drill another hole of the same size on the opposite long side. Push the pvc pipe through both holes in the mold. Insert the pvc pipe through the mold in the hole.

10 Cut any excess pipe; it should protrude about an inch from either side of the mold.

[Casting the sidepieces]

1 Cut the rebar into four pieces that are each 1.2 m in length. Bend the rebars to fit into the mold. The rebars should not touch the edges of the mold.

2 Place the mold on a flat surface so that it is perfectly level; check that it is flat with a spirit level.

3 Mix the concrete according to the instructions on the bag. Fill the mold halfway with concrete. Put the two bent rebars in the mold, parallel to the long sides.

4 Fill the mold with concrete. Mix the concrete with a trowel. Tap with a rebar to remove the air bubbles (see the tip on page 143).

5 When the mold is completely filled, smooth the surface of the concrete with the trowel. Secure the mold with some clamps.

6 Gently tap the walls of the mold with a rubber mallet to remove any remaining air bubbles from the wet concrete.

7 Cover the mold with plastic sheeting and let the concrete cure for 4–5 days.

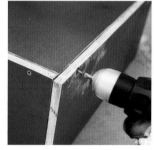

8 Unscrew the mold and gently detach the concrete.

9 Clean the mold with soapy water, and cast the second side panel. Allow the concrete to cure for four to five days before assembling the bench.

10 When the concrete is fully cured, use a rubber mallet to gently knock the pvc pipes from the side panels.

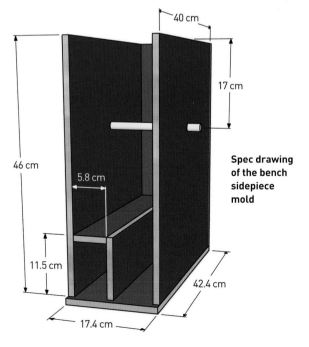

40 cm

17 cm

5.8 cm

46 cm

11.5 cm

42.4 cm

17.4 cm

Spec drawing of the bench sidepiece mold

[Building the paving stone base]

1 Choose where the bench will stand, and with the marking sticks, mark off an area of 80 x 160 cm. Remove the soil; be sure to dig down at least 30 cm into the soil. Cover the hole with the ground cloth and fill it with gravel. Use a soil compactor to vibrate the gravel. Check the surface with a spirit level to confirm that it is flat.

2 Place the stone tiles on the compacted surface. Arrange the stones so the outer edges are as straight as possible and so the stones are equally spaced.

3 Build a frame from the wooden planks and screw them together with brackets.

4 Adjust the stones to lie flat and level by removing or adding gravel as needed. Use an angle grinder to re-shape the stones if they don't fit properly.

5 Brush the paving sand between the stones. Water with a spray nozzle so the paving sand is soaked through completely. Allow the paving sand to dry for 8 hours before starting on the next step.

6 Remove the wooden frame and cut away any visible ground cloth. Fill the border around the stone tiles with gravel.

Spec drawing of the finished bench

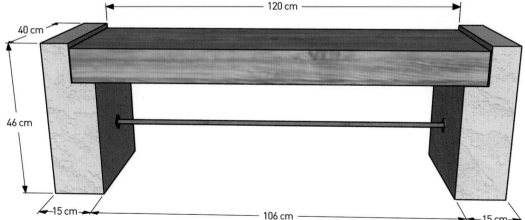

120 cm

40 cm

46 cm

15 cm

106 cm

15 cm

[Assemble the bench]

1 The paving sand will be fully dry after three days and the bench can be assembled. Position the bench's sidepieces on the paving stones; they should stand parallel to each other and make sure the distance between them is correct (see spec drawing of the finished bench on the bottom left).

2 If the iron pipe is too long, cut it to 106 cm. The pipe will sit between the sidepieces.

3 With a joint nut, piece together the two threaded rods. The joined rod should be at least 1.6 m long. The joined rod should run freely through the pipe.

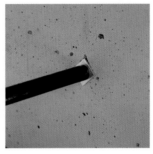

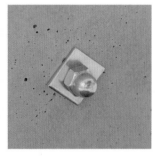

4 Screw an additional joint nut onto the joined rod approximately 80 cm from the first joint nut. The nuts act as spacers to keep the rod centered in the pipe.

5 Push the joined rod through the hole on the outside of one of the bench's sidepieces. When the rod comes out the other side, slide on a square washer. Align the rod in the iron pipe.

6 When the rod comes out of the pipe, screw on another square washer at that end. Continue to push the rod through the hole in the other sidepiece.

7 Cut both sides of the rod so that it protrudes only about 1 cm from the cement side panels. Screw on square washers and finish by screwing on a cap nut against the sidepiece's outside.

8 Use a ruler to check that the concrete side panels are parallel to each other.

9 Cut the solid wooden plank to the required length. Optionally, you can treat the wood with copperas to quickly give the wood that aged, silver hue (see tip p. 85).

10 Place the plank between the side panels. The bench is ready.

CHAPTER No 3

CARPENTRY

Nature—a treasure trove

In several of the book's woodworking projects, I use natural, untreated wood, which is a beautiful material and one that's great to work with. In this chapter, there is a tool rack built of driftwood, birch trunks crafted into a partition, and a chair made of pine branches; these projects have allowed me to adapt to the natural shapes and textures of the wood. For other projects, I use finished lumber of various dimensions, which is easy to use and quick to build with.

Many of us have built tree houses from wooden scraps, but even some historic castles have been made of wood. Sweden's Ekebyhov Castle is a well-preserved wooden castle from the late 1600s.

It's difficult to find a building material more natural than wood. Wood has a surprisingly long life, can be recycled, and has its own natural cycle. Different types of wood show great variation in their qualities. Color, texture, durability, density, hardness, and strength are just some of the characteristics that vary between types of wood. In the olden days, peasants and craftsmen had a deep, cultural knowledge of different woods and their various functions—a knowledge that migrated and evolved through the generations. When they made wooden tines, they used lilac wood. Ash, which is resilient and strong, is still used today to make oars, tool handles, and dog sledges. Alder is worked into shape easily and can absorb moisture well, and therefore it makes great clogs. Matches are made of aspen, which is a light wood without resin.

The Age of a Tree

Some tree species are fast growing while others are slow growing. Oak is one of the longest-lived trees in the world, and can grow for a thousand years or more, while aspen does not live beyond a hundred years. You can find out the age of a tree by counting the trunk's annual rings. These cells grow differently depending on the seasons.

This 30 cm-thick tree was 59 years old when it fell. The maximum age for a pine is about 400 years.

This Scots pine was only 20 cm in diameter, but even so, it was 85 years old. Scots pines can live up to 800 years.

Rings that grow in the spring are lighter in color and are called "springwood." Toward the end of the summer darker rings form and are called "summerwood." In some tree species, such as aspen, it is difficult to discern annual rings, while the pine's and Scots pine's growth rings tend to be easier to count.

From Log to Plank

During large-scale logging, tree trunks are picked up by timber trucks and delivered to a sawmill where the logs are sawn into the appropriate dimensions. For small-scale logging, mobile sawmills are used. The sawmill is sent out to the courtyard, and the logs are sawn up on site. After they are sawn, the planks must be dried. At the lumber yard, freshly sawn timber is laid flat and aired during the stacking process, when the sun and wind removes water from the wood.

Wood shrinks when water evaporates. Shrinkage occurs differently in different areas in the wood, and the tensions that build up may cause the wood to crack or twist. Depending on how a plank is sawn from the log, shape differences will appear between the boards. A plank that is sawn from the center of the tree may shrink uniformly and have only small shape changes, while a board sawn from the outer edge of the tree will have relatively large changes in shape.

The moisture content is higher in the outer edge than in the heartwood, which means that planks sawn from the outer parts of the tree will shrink more than heartwood. By looking at the rings, one can predict how the plank will change in shape when it dries.

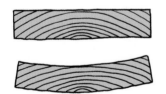

A plank tends to become concave if the heartwood is facing downward when it dries during the stacking process. Correspondingly, the plank becomes convex if the heartwood is facing upwards. If the planks are screwed onto the underlying joists instead of nailed, they retain their shape better.

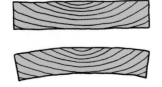

Stakes of juniper, oak, dense-growing fir, and pine have been used to make fences for a long time. Sometimes the tips are charred or tarred to protect them from rotting, but often they are used untreated. When the bottom end is rotten, it can be trimmed off and reused. This beautiful old fence is surrounded by flowering pansies.

Trees on Trees

For generations, forests have been planted for specific purposes. One of the most famous historical examples was the careful cultivation of over 300,000 oaks in the beginning of the 1800s in Visingsö, with the idea that the wood could be harvested several hundred years later for boat construction. Today, we plant fast-growing willows of the genus *Salix* on arable land to mine energy. Energy forests are usually felled in 3–5 years.

screws are placed close to the end grain of the plank.

Treating the wood with paint, oil, or tar will prolong its lifespan significantly. In crafts, wood is often transformed into beautiful utilitarian and art pieces.

Buying Lumber

In many of the projects in this book, a beam or wooden sheet is required. The lumberyard has many different lumber sizes and grades, and it can sometimes be difficult to find what you are looking for.

Besides looking for lumber of the right dimensions, you must also ensure that they are the right lengths. Wood is bought in standard lengths, so one must assume that there will always be leftover wood. Bring a list of the lengths you will need and buy pieces in the size that will produce the least waste.

Wide Range of Applications

The easiest way to build with wood is to use narrow trunks and branches without any special processing. When thicker tree trunks are sawn into planks of varying dimensions, the field of use is large. Timber is used in frame structures as well as fitments and joinery, while planks made from compressed wood fibers or particles are suitable for all kinds of uses.

You can glue, nail, and assemble wooden structures. If you choose to use screws, then it's good to use self-tapping screws or to pre-drill holes for screws to ensure that the wood won't crack. This is particularly important if

DRIFTWOOD TOOL RACK

Items such as machinery, planting pots, seed boxes, and willow trellises should be stored in the garden shed. However, it's not always convenient to walk over to the shed to fetch a tool you need, and these are often left lying out by the flowerbed or wherever they were last used. So they're not where they're supposed to be, and the long search begins—where did I put the shovel? It usually takes one or two laps around the garden to locate the lost shovel. This annoyance can easily be avoided. The tools that I use most often have their own easily-accessed place outside the shed—hanging on a tool rack. This tool rack is made from two materials of aged character: driftwood and hand-forged nails. The silver-gray wood and the black, slightly rough iron nails warm my heart.

MATERIALS

- 1 piece of driftwood (120 x 1100 mm)
- 1 wall stud (45 x 70 x 650 mm)
- 2 brackets (75 x 19 x 2 mm)
- 5 hand-forged nails (5 x 120 mm)
- 2 decking screws (4.8 x 55 mm)
- 8 wood screws (4 x 40 mm)

TOOLS

- Directional board
- Jigsaw
- Utility knife
- Drill driver
- Drill bits (3 mm and 5 mm)
- Hacksaw
- Spirit level
- Hammer

STEP BY STEP

Getting a hold of a piece of driftwood may not be easy. If you want to make a tool rack that has the beautiful silver-gray color of aged wood but you don't have driftwood, you can treat fresh, untreated lumber with copperas (see tip on page 85). Use a wood with a rough surface.

1 Measure the wood stud that will be attached to the back of the driftwood and placed against the wall. Make sure it fits. If it is too big, cut it down to size, so it doesn't stick out from behind the driftwood.

2 Place the front side of the board against the wood stud. Fasten the driftwood and wood stud to the workbench so that the driftwood sticks out equally on both sides. The driftwood and the wood stud should both be uniformly thick in order for the driftwood to hang nicely on the wall.

3 Place the wood stud parallel to the workbench's edge against the driftwood's backside. Measure the largest gap between the driftwood and the stud. In my case it was 8 mm. Copy the contour of the driftwood to the stud by bringing the folding ruler along the driftwood simultaneously as you hold a pen at the 8 mm line on the folding ruler.

4 Saw and trim away the material from the stud according to the marks so that the ruler and driftwood are equally thick. Fasten them to the workbench and verify the total thickness.

5 Pre-drill 2 holes with a 3 mm drill through the stud, about 10 cm from the stud's short sides. Screw the stud together with the driftwood on the backside of the stud.

6 Pre-drill 5 holes with a 5 mm drill through the driftwood for the iron nails. Distribute the holes evenly on the board and make sure they do not completely go through the stud. Drill the holes so that the nails lean upwards. This way, the tools will hang steadily on the nails. Put the nails in the holes and make sure they sit on a straight line.

7 Cut the brackets so that they fit on the backside of the tool board. Pre-drill with a 3 mm drill and screw the brackets into the stud, 5 cm from the stud's short sides. Then, screw the tool rack on the wall. Check with a spirit level that the tool rack sits horizontally.

8 Hammer the iron nails into the pre-drilled holes. Make sure they are secured. The tool rack is ready to be used.

HOP POLE

Nature's vigorous growth is fascinating. As a child, I was delighted by the hop plant's fast rampage up all the hop poles. It was almost as if I could watch the hops grow each time I looked at them. Making a hop pole is a simple and fun garden project and it offers quick rewards. Following the hops as they make their way to the top of pole is fun for both children and adults. We made our hop pole out of recycled materials. The pole itself began as a flagpole from the children's old playhouse, and it was ready for a new assignment.

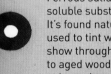

Help Nature Along

Ferrous sulfate, also known as copperas, is a water-soluble substance with the chemical formula $FeSO_4$. It's found naturally in certain minerals and can be used to tint wood. The structure of the wood will show through, and the surface will become similar to aged wood. Ferrous sulfate can be purchased at home improvement stores in powder or crystal form. Dissolve the powder in water according to the instructions on the package.

MATERIALS

- 1 long pole of 6 m (60 mm thick)
- Copperas
- 1 ground anchor (50 x 50 mm)
- 1 decoration for the top
- Two screws (4 x 40 mm)

TOOLS

- Paint scraper (if the pole is painted)
- Brush
- Saw
- Knife or chisel
- Hammer
- Sledgehammer
- Wooden block
- Spirit level
- Drill driver
- Drill bit (3 mm)
- Spade

PLANTS

- Golden Hop, *Humulus lupulus* 'Aureus' (1 pc)
- White Navelwort, *Omphalodes verna* 'Alba' (5 pcs)

STEP BY STEP

Carefully select where you want to place your hop pole. Hops grow incredibly vigorously, and if they get the opportunity, they can grow over garden beds, bicycles, and other things standing nearby. Hops can even smother other vegetation if they're left unmanaged. Hops thrive in deep, processed, and fertile soil. Nurture the soil with compost if you want the hops to grow lushly.

1 Prepare a long straight pole. The taller the pole, the more exciting it will be to watch. Our old white-stained flagpole by the playground was a 6 m long pine pole, from which I scraped off the paint.

2 Treat the pole with copperas and it will soon turn a silver-gray (see tip on page 85).

3 Make sure the pole fits into the ground anchor. Our pole was a little too wide to fit. Mark the height of the ground anchor around the pole.

4 Cut four evenly distributed slots around the pole by the mark made in step 3.

5 Use a sharp knife or chisel and peel off the wood along the sides up to the slots. Check regularly if the pole fits the anchor so that you do not peel away too much.

6 Place a decoration at the top of the pole. We reused the ball that graced the top of the old flagpole.

7 Insert a block of wood into the ground anchor as protection and knock the anchor down into the ground where the hop pole will stand.

8 Remove the wooden block and insert the hop pole into the ground anchor. Check with a spirit level to confirm that the pole is straight. Pre-drill holes in the pole for the screws. Screw the hop pole to the ground anchor.

9 Plant hops beside the pole. Water them and watch how the hops begin to work their way toward the top. You may need to redirect the shoots back to the pole if they're trying to climb onto something else.

10 Blue-eyed Marys work well as ground covering vegetation with the hops. In the beginning of the summer, they produce flowers similar to those of the Forget-me-not. Very soon, their shoots will grow together and will spread to cover the earth.

BIRCH SAPLING PARTITION

Many houses have a long side or wall that is completely smooth and has no protruding stairs, balconies, or other structures. Nothing is there to catch the eye and the wall can feel bare and uninviting. The back of our house was just like this. Our '80s house has a long flat wall facing north with a wide soffit. Not many plants are happy in these conditions. Instead of being a cozy place where we could enjoy the evening sun, our back wall had become an eyesore. An easy way to visually shorten one side of the empty wall is to put up a divider so you can't see the entirety of the long wall at once. My simple partition is built from narrow birch trunks.

MATERIALS

- 5 birch saplings (4–8 cm in diameter)
- 5 galvanized eye bolts (30 x 12 mm)
- 5 galvanized screw hooks (length 50 mm)
- 2 rebar at 70 cm (8 mm)

TOOLS

- Saw
- Ruler
- Drill driver
- Drill bits (4 mm and 8 mm)
- Ladder
- Hammer
- Clamps
- Bolt cutter

Betula

STEP BY STEP

Birch saplings and other leafy trees make excellent screens and partitions. They need to be narrow and relatively straight. Check how many saplings you need. In my case, I needed five; I used one sapling per eave board.

1 Trim the birch trunks so they are 10 cm shorter than the distance between the eaves and the ground. Pre-drill a hole with a 4 mm drill in the middle of the top edge of each birch trunk.

2 Screw the eye bolts in the pre-drilled holes so that the eye almost touches the birch trunk.

3 Mark the place on the overhang of the roof where you want to insert the hooks. Drill holes at the marks with a 4 mm drill.

4 Screw the hooks into the eaves. Hang the birch saplings on the hooks.

5 Use two horizontal rebars to hold the logs together. Select the height where the rebars should run across. Start with the lower hinge. Drill a horizontal hole into the outer birch sapling with a 8 mm drill.

6 Hammer the rebar through the first birch sapling so that it reaches the next sapling. Mark the rebar where it should hit the next log. Move the outer birch sapling away so that you can drill a horizontal hole at the mark in the second trunk.

7 Continue in the same way with other trunks until the rebar has been inserted through all of them. Proceed similarly with the upper rebar; this time you'll have to remove one birch sapling from its hook at a time, and hold it to the side so you can drill the holes.

8 Use two clamps to adjust the distance between the birch saplings; they should hang vertically and be evenly spread over the bars.

9 Remove the screw clamps. Trim any excess rebar; only 1–2 cm should protrude on either side of the outer birch saplings. The partition is done.

GARDEN BOX

Picking fresh lettuce, crispy carrots, and sweet peas straight from the vegetable garden makes for an inspired cook and meal. However, this can be troublesome if the conditions are not just right. Heavy loam is nutritious but too compact for vegetables to thrive in. Since rocky soil does not usually produce good conditions for plants, a stand-alone garden box is perfect. Place the box in the sun, fill it with nutritious soil, water it regularly, and you'll be rewarded with a vegetable garden that yields a great harvest and is easy to manage. A good tip is to plant a few small summer flowers among the vegetables. It looks beautiful and you can pick a floral bouquet for the dinner table while you harvest the vegetables for your meal.

MATERIALS

Makes a box 1.4 x 3 m.
- 38 m raw cut boards (22 x 95 mm)
- 4.2 m wall stud (45 x 45 mm)
- Approx. 100 wood screws (4 x 55 mm)
- Wood screws (4 x 40 mm) to join the boards
- 1 liter water-based wood stain
- 5 m² black plant cover
- 1.5 m³ planting and compost soil

TOOLS

- Yardstick or tape measure
- Saw
- Ax
- Screwdriver
- Brush
- Spirit level
- Sledgehammer
- Scissors
- Spade
- Rake
- Wheelbarrow

STEP BY STEP

Find a sunny spot in your garden that's large enough for your garden box. If possible, place the garden box close to the kitchen, so you have a real kitchen garden. Measure out the preferred dimensions for your garden box and gather all the materials. My box is placed on a slope and is therefore three boards high at the back end and four boards high at the front.

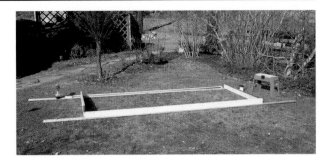

1 Cut the first 4–7 boards to the required length (see the drawing on the next page) and shape them into a base frame. I had to make oblique cuts for the bottom sideboards as the box is standing on a slope.

2 Glaze all the surfaces that will soon be hidden with copperas or paint to treat the wood.

3 Screw together the bottom of the frame and place it in its designated location. Use a spirit level to check that it's straight.

4 Cut the wood stud into five 55 cm-long pieces and three 45 cm-long pieces. Form one end of each piece into a spike, so you can insert them easily into the ground where they will stay. Put two long stays or upright supports in the inside corners of the front of the box and two short stays (or upright supports) in the back corners. Hammer the corner stays about 15 cm into the soil and screw the box wall and the corner stays together. The stays stabilize and anchor the box in the ground. I had some leftover lumber of triangular studs, which I put in the corners, but you can also use square studs.

5 My box was so long that it needed extra stays. Hammer a short stay down in the middle of the box's edge and distribute the three additional long stays along the inside of the front edge. Screw the wall of the garden box to the stays.

6 It's possible to splice the boards to make the box wall. If you choose to do this, insert a piece of wood on the inside of the box's wall and screw the boards with 40 mm screws.

7 Cut the stays on a line with the top of the garden box. Slope the top edge of the stays a bit, or screw a piece of wood onto the stay, as decoration and protection from the rain. Glaze the box's inside and outside.

8 Dig away the turf in the box and line the base with newspapers. Cover the gaps between the boards with a black plant cover so the soil is better able to stay in place.

9 Fill the box with nutritious garden or compost soil. I built the foundation for the soil with material from rabbit hutches.

10 The top layer of the soil should be 20 cm deep with fine garden or compost soil.

11 Mark straight seed rows with a straight stick. Water the rows before planting the seeds so they can germinate faster.

12 Planting the seeds in straight lines makes it easy to clear out and weed. I put a row of strawberry plants in the front and clumps of chives in one corner.

13 Remember to mark the rows properly. This will help when it's time to clean out the garden box.

14 After a few weeks the seeds will have germinated, and there will be a row of small plants in the garden box.

Important Dimensions

You can make your garden box as long as you like. Typically, the length of the box is determined by the space available in your garden. However, the width is also important. In order to be able to reach your plants from all directions, the garden box shouldn't be wider than 1.5 m. This way you can reach everything without needing to step into the box. When placing a garden box against an existing wall or a fence, it shouldn't be wider than 90 cm. The box needs to be at least 30 cm tall for the carrots and other deep-growing vegetables, so the roots can thrive.

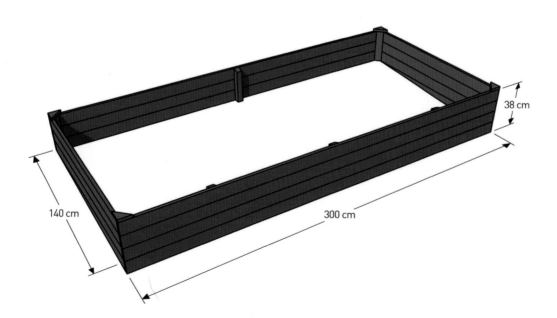

Spec drawing of the garden box

38 cm

140 cm

300 cm

Annual Malope,
Malope trifida

Zinnia, *Zinnia elegans*

Cornflower, *Centaurea cyanus*

Marigold, *Calendula officinalis*

Cosmos, *Cosmos bipinnatus* 'Purity'

Fill the Box with Your Favorites

For me, it's important to have access to fresh dill, parsley, and chives. So of course, they have a permanent place in my box. I also like to have something to nibble whenever I clear out the garden box and care for my plants; my row of strawberry plants produce sun-warmed berries that I can pop directly in my mouth.

Different kinds of beets—'Forono,' 'Moulin Rouge,' and 'Chioggia'—are three varieties that produce fine, healthy vegetables. 'Chioggia' is called the candy-striped beet and is striped like a candy cane. It tastes like regular beetroot, but it's more beautiful on the plate. The garden box also needs a few rows of summer and winter carrots.

For peas and beans, I chose the taller varieties. These provide a plentiful harvest and only take up a small area. Sow the beans in a

20 cm large square. All you need is to sow two bean plants in each corner. If both bean plants germinate, cut away one of them so there's only one bean plant per corner. Place long sticks in the soil beside the seedlings and tie them together at the top to give the beans a good frame to climb on.

Growing onions is also rewarding work. The easiest and fastest way to do this is to buy small onion bulbs in the spring rather than sowing seeds. I grow leeks in a similar manner. Instead of pre-growing the leeks indoors, I buy a box of seedlings from the nursery. Then, all I have to do is distribute the seedlings in the garden box. Lastly, I leave room for summer flowers. These break up the green with a symphony of colors. More than this, they're rewarding to grow—the more flowers you pick the more you'll get.

Tree Mallow, *Lavatera trimestris* 'Silver Cup'

Care and Growing Advice

Your vegetables need water and nutrition to grow. Water them at least once a week if it's been dry and sunny for a long time. Loosen up the earth's surface after rain or watering so the soil will better retain moisture.

A garden box elevates the plants and the edge prevents most weeds from penetrating the box. The stray weed that does get in can easily be plucked.

If you want to enjoy small delicate vegetables early in the season, you should cull your plants twice. Once the seeds have germinated and the delicate plants are growing close to their lines,

it is time to cull a first time. Don't thin them out too much—leave a smaller distance between younger seedlings than you would leave for fully-grown plants. After a few weeks you can harvest every other vegetable and leave more space for the remaining plants to grow big.

To prevent the earth from becoming depleted, you'll need to stock up on plant food. This can be done easily and naturally with grass clippings. Introducing a 5 cm-thick layer twice per season is quite enough. Clippings provide nitrogen to the plants and also help the soil better retain moisture.

PINE BRANCH CHAIR

Putting nature's offerings to use is something that's very attractive. My friend Eva passionately told me about the beautiful garden furniture her family had when she was a child; it was all made of gnarled branches. The thought of furniture made out of branches appealed to me. After an autumn storm, several trees had fallen around our house. The logs were put to use, but the branches would have been thrown out or burned for fire wood. I saved a few and built myself a rustic chair. While it has no straight lines, the chair is comfortable, rugged, and very charming. It looks right at home in the corner of the garden by the blueberry bushes, beside the small pond.

MATERIALS

- 10–15 pine branches (2–6 cm in diameter)
- 20–30 self-drilling decking screws (30–90 mm)
- 1 wooden plank (40 x 400 x 400 mm)

TOOLS

- Pruning saw
- Quick-grip clamps
- String or straps
- Utility knife
- Drill driver
- Drill bit (3 mm)
- Jigsaw
- Spirit level
- Sander
- Sandpaper

Let the Chair Evolve

When building a chair out of tree branches, you can't really follow a detailed spec drawing. Instead, you'll have to work with the material and allow the chair to grow organically, step by step. It's easier to see what the chair will ultimately look like if you tie its parts together with string and straps at the beginning. If you're not satisfied with the shape, you'll have to look for branches that fit together better.

Pinus sylvestris

STEP BY STEP

Oak and pine branches are usually crooked and gnarled and excellent to make a chair out of. Since pine trees had fallen around our house, pine branches were the obvious choice. If you can't get a solid 40 cm-wide plank, you can also build the seat with thinner wood.

1 Choose two branches of equal thickness that are naturally bent; these will serve as front legs and side-pieces. Piece these together with branches between the legs and the rear. Make sure the legs are a little longer than needed so there is the possibility to adjust them by cutting them down to size.

2 Select two fairly straight branches for the cross-bars that the seat will rest on. A crossbar should sit between the front and back legs.

3 Disassemble the chair and remove the bark on the branches with a knife.

4 Reassemble the branches and tie the chair together with string.

5 Cut a piece of paper to be approximately the same shape as the frame's outer line. Insert the paper under the frame and attach it with clamps.

6 Draw the frame's inner edge on the paper template.

7 Remove the template from the frame. Draw a second line on the paper about 2 cm outside the first one. Cut the paper template at the outer line.

8 Turn the plank so the growth rings point up (otherwise the seat will become bowl-shaped when it settles (read more on p 80)).

9 Mark the paper template's outer lines on the plank and cut the seat with a jigsaw.

10 Angle the blade on the jigsaw to a 45° angle.

11 Miter the top edge on the seat's back and side edges.

12 On the seat, mark out how much wood must be removed to insert one of the legs. Cut; test to see if the leg fits in the hole. Deepen the hole as needed. Mark the hole for the next leg and cut it out. Repeat for all legs.

13 Place the seat on the crossbars and tie it together with string and straps.

14 Try to fit the seat into the frame. Mark the points where the seat must be tweaked and trim it until you are satisfied.

15 Use self-tapping screws and fasten the seat to the top edge of the frame.

16 Ensure that the crossbars rest firmly against the seat. Screw the crossbars to the legs. Also screw together the chair's legs, the backside edge, and the side branches so that the legs are sturdy.

17 Screw the seat into the two crossbars from below.

18 Put spacers under the chair's legs so that the seat is horizontal. Check both directions with a spirit level.

19 Trim off any parts of the legs that are too long so the chair is level.

20 Sand the seat until it becomes smooth. If you can't get a hold of an electric sander, use sandpaper.

21 Choose two rounded branches to make the arm rests. Remove the bark and cut the branches to fit the chair. Screw the arm rests into the frame.

22 Finally, screw in a lightly bent branch that has been stripped of bark to decorate the back of the stool. Cut off any little branches that stick out and the chair is done!

JAPANESE-INSPIRED TRELLIS

When traveling around the world, I find myself attracted to beautiful old structures. A structure that has been etched into my memory is the traditional Japanese gate called the torii (pronounced with a long "e"). The word means 'gate' in Japanese. Torii are large and stately, and they traditionally lead into Shinto shrines or sacred natural places. A classic torii has two vertical columns and two horizontal lintels. Although my trellis is made to be a climbing frame and a screen between the neighbor's yard and mine, the color and diagonally cut top also give a little hint of Japan. This trellis is built from wood and steel mesh and is simple in its design.

MATERIALS

- 2 ground anchors (70 x 70 mm)
- 7.4 m flat planed lumber (70 x 70 mm)
- 1 mesh with 20 x 20 cm square pattern (145 x 165 cm)
- 0.5 liter of oil-based wood stain (English red)
- 0.5 liter black metal paint
- 4 brackets (50 x 50 x 35 mm)
- 32 wood screws (4 x 40 mm)
- 16 staples
- 8 French wood screws (10 x 50 mm)

TOOLS

- Sledgehammer
- Ruler
- Saw
- Clamps
- Spirit level
- Corner clamp
- Brush
- Sponges
- Drill driver
- Drill bits (3 mm and 9 mm)
- Hammer
- Socket wrench (for the French wood screws)
- Masking tape

STEP BY STEP

Reinforcement nets make very useful climbing frames for plants. Clematis, especially, likes to spin its petioles around the brackets and will quickly fill up a large area. If you want to build a longer trellis, you'll need several vertical posts that are anchored in the ground. The distance between the posts should not be wider than 160 cm, so the trellis will be stable and steady.

1 Place the ground anchors where the trellis posts are to stand. Put a block of wood in the ground anchor so it doesn't get damaged when you hammer it. Hammer the ground anchor into the ground so it stands steady.

2 Insert the posts into the ground anchors and clamp the top rail with screw clamps. Use a spirit level to ensure that it lies flat. Mark the posts where they should be cut.

3 Cut the poles by the marks and miter the header at 60 degrees. Cut the wood stud at the bottom of the trellis to fit between the posts.

4 Test-mount the trellis by holding the poles and mesh with screw clamps. The reinforcing mesh is attached to the back of the trellis. It should overlap on the wooden posts so there will be plenty of space for securing the net to the posts.

5 Disassemble the trellis and paint the wood studs red.

6 Paint the reinforcing mesh with black metal paint. Dip a sponge into the paint to better paint the iron (read more to the right).

7 Also paint the brackets, staples, and heads on the French screws with black metal paint.

8 Screw the brackets onto the underside of the horizontal wood stud. Drill the holes so that the wood does not crack.

9 Reassemble the trellis. Hold the parts together with screw clamps.

10 Fasten the spirit level against one of the posts with a screw clamp and make sure that the trellis is straight, both horizontally and vertically.

11 If necessary, align the wooden frame so that it is parallel with the reinforcing mesh.

12 Place brackets under the crossbars and pre-drill the holes. Screw the brackets to the inside of the posts and the crossbars' underside. Fasten the lower stud to the trellis in the same manner as the brackets on the underside of the stud.

13 Use staples to attach the reinforcing mesh to the backside of the wooden frame.

14 Drill with 9 mm drill and fasten the posts into the ground anchors with French screws. Mark the drilling depth with masking tape on the drill to get the correct depth. Angle the screw holes slightly so that the screws do not meet in the middle.

15 Screw the pole into the ground anchor with French screws. Check regularly with a spirit level to ensure that the pole is straight.

Painting Reinforcement Mesh

Many like the rusty color that reinforcement mesh gets when it's left untreated. Others think it looks better as a glossy black. Sometimes it can be tricky to paint all around the steel mesh. A convenient way is to hang it in a tree and paint it. When the net hangs freely, it's easier to access all the surfaces from both the front and back, and to check if the color covers the brackets. Use a sponge to apply the paint; it's much smoother than using a brush.

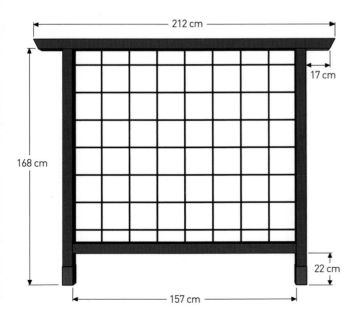

212 cm

17 cm

168 cm

22 cm

157 cm

Spec drawing of the Japanese-inspired trellis

A SWING FOR TWO

As a little girl, one of my favorite things to do was to swing. In the middle of the garden stood a huge, old apple tree that we called the "cranky stump." The trunk was partially hollow and just like Pippi Longstocking, we stored our soda in the tree. A swing was attached to a branch high above the ground, and we would swing as fast and as high as we could. It was delightful to feel the breeze in our hair and butterflies in our stomachs as we swung back down from a great height. A classic swing still creates warm feelings of nostalgia. Today, my swing is attached to a big branch high up in a large oak. The swing has room for two—a wonderful combination of nostalgia and romance.

Take Care of Your Tree

In order not to damage the branch of the tree, I attached the swing's ropes to a wide strap that runs across the branch. The strap is gentler on the branch than rope, which would cut into the bark. The strap distributes the weight of the swing so the underlying growth layer (cambium) isn't damaged.

MATERIALS

Makes a swing that is attached 7.5 m up in the tree.

- 1 planed wooden plank (45 x 195 x 1100 mm)
- 47 cm flat bars of steel (30 x 3 mm)
- Copperas
- 4 loop nuts M8
- 4 M8 bolts (60 mm)
- 8 washers M8
- 32 m 3-battle cordage (14 mm)
- 4 snap hooks with eyelet (80 mm)
- 4 locking carabiner (100 mm)
- 12 m synthetic tape (50 mm)
- 4 buckles for strap
- 8 m double braided scout rope (12 mm)
- Tape, for example Tesa (19 or 38 mm)

TOOLS

- 20 m light string with a weight attached, for example, a small cloth bag filled with sand
- Ruler
- Saw
- Angle grinder
- Bending machine or vise and pipe wrench
- Chisels
- Drill driver
- Drill bit (9 mm)
- Fretsaw or utility knife
- Countersink bit
- Sander or sandpaper
- Wrench
- Split needles
- 20 m rope, e.g. a flagpole rope

STEP BY STEP

Start by measuring the height of the selected branch to find out how much rope is needed. Then, check that the branch is strong enough to hold the weight. It should be able to bear the weight of two adults. I have chosen 3-battle cordage to be the safety rope. By splicing the rope, the fastening loops will become both beautiful and durable.

1 Hold the loose rope end and throw the weight over the branch. Pull back the string to stretch it, so that the weight hovers just above the ground. Make a mark on the string level with the ground and measure the string's length.

2 Prepare the support rails of the flat bar. Cut it into two parts so that each one is 23.5 cm long. Bend both ends of the bar at a 90-degree angle, 2.5 cm from the edge. Then cut a 105 cm-long wooden plank, if it is not already the right length.

3 Cut and carve out 2 tracks, which are 0.5 cm deep and 3.5 cm wide at the seat's bottom, so that the support rails can be folded into the board. Place the tracks 5 cm from the seat's edges. Drill a hole through the support rail and the seat half an inch away from the seat's long sides.

4 Round off the seat edges at the top until smooth, so that no splinters are sticking out. It can be done with a hand-held plunge router. If not, carve the edges with a knife.

5 Bevel the drilled holes in the seat on the upper side so that the screws are countersunk.

6 Sand the board with a sander or sandpaper so that the surface becomes soft and smooth.

7 Treat the board with copperas (see tip on page 85); to get a natural graying color from the beginning.

8 Bring out loop nuts, bolts, and four washers to each side when the surface dries.

9 Mount the support rails to the seat's bottom. Put a washer between the bolt and rail and between the screw and loop nuts on the seat's top. Secure the loops properly.

10 The seat is finished. Safely attach the ropes to the loops.

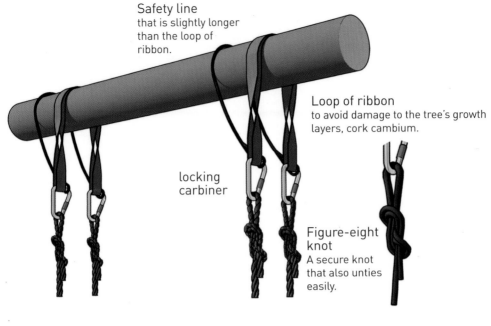

Safety line
that is slightly longer than the loop of ribbon.

Loop of ribbon
to avoid damage to the tree's growth layers, cork cambium.

locking carbiner

Figure-eight knot
A secure knot that also unties easily.

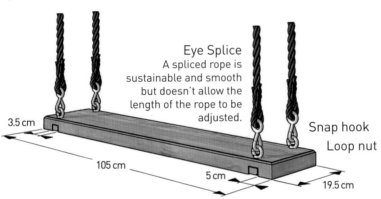

Eye Splice
A spliced rope is sustainable and smooth but doesn't allow the length of the rope to be adjusted.

Snap hook
Loop nut

3.5 cm

105 cm

5 cm

19.5 cm

To prevent the branch from being damaged, the swing's ropes are mounted with locking carabiners on a broad strap, which is placed on top of the branch. I also attached an additional rope to act as a safety line. It goes parallel to the strap on the top of the branch. The strap will be shorter than the safety line.

[Make a loop of ribbon with a safety rope]

1 To mount the swing you need a loop of ribbon and a safety line for each side. Start by cutting the synthetic strap in two parts. Take one part and make the first loop. Slide the buckles onto the belt ends. Tie a loose knot outside the buckle on one end of the ribbon so that there is an approximately 30 cm band hanging from the knot.

2 Insert the second end of the strap through the loose knot so the buckles end up on each side. Adjust the strap so that the loop is about 2 m long.

3 Insert the loose strap ends through the buckles and tape the straps together at the side of the knot.

4 Tighten the knot so that it is properly secured.

5 Tape the loose strap ends to the band with Tesa tape.

6 Attach the two locking carabiners to the belt loop and tape the band below the carbines. Cut the double braided rope in half. Take one string and make one eight-knot with a loop at each end (see spec drawing on the previous page). Attach the safety line to the locking carabiners so that it hangs parallel to the belt loop. The string should be 30 cm longer than the band. Adjust the length if necessary. Make the next one in the same way.

[Splice the battle cordage]

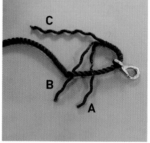

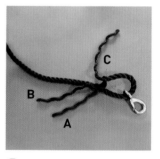

1 Cut the battle cordage into four parts. Splice one suspension rope at a time. Pass the line through the carbine loop. Wrap the rope with a thin string, 20 cm and 40 cm in from the rope's end.

2 Separate the strands of the first band and spread them as shown in the picture. Insert the middle strand (B) perpendicular to a strand of the cord, just above the second knot.

3 Remove the lower strand (A) and insert it to the left of the first strand (B).

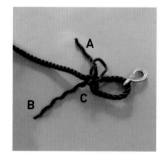

4 Flip the rope so the bottom comes up. Stick the third strand (C) between the first two tucks, from right to left. The first row of the splice is complete.

5 Continue in the same way "over one and under one." With a split pin it is easier to insert the strands through the rope.

6 In order to obtain a strong splice five plugins are needed. Finish the splice by cutting the string ends. You can also make a tapered splice by removing some yarn from each strand before the end. Make the other three suspension lines in the same way. Make an eight-knot with a loop at the rope's other end (see diagram on previous page).

[Mount the swing in the tree]

The last step is to mount the swing in the tree. If the branch sits high, it is both difficult and dangerous to climb the tree. It is better to mount the swing from the ground; just make sure that you know in what order the ropes are to go up into the tree. Follow the diagrams below.

1 Throw the weight that is attached to the lightweight rope over the branch where the swing will hang.

2 Remove the weight and tie the more powerful rope instead (highlighted green) to the string. Pull back the lightweight rope (marked in red) over branch. Remove the light string.

3 Start by linking two of the suspension ropes upside down on each side of the band loop, meaning, connect the carbines with the spliced loop to the locking carabiner in the string. Let the end with the eight-knot hang free. Attach one of the eight-knots to the battle cordage (highlighted green) and pull it over the branch.

4 Adjust the length of the suspension lines by adjusting the eight-knots, and measure exactly where they should sit so that the swing will hang at the right height. Tighten the eight-knots when the alignment is made.

5 Now, the suspension lines should be correctly positioned. The eight-knots should sit in the locking carabiner. Attach one of the free snap hooks to the battle cordage (marked in green) and pull back through the rope so that the battle cordage hangs on each side of the branch.

6 Disconnect the string. Now, one of the suspension lines is in place and has the right length. Proceed in the same way with the ropes on the other side of the swing. Lastly, hook the seat on.

CHAPTER

One

LAYING STONE AND MOSAIC

My love for stone

Natural stone is one of my absolute favorite materials for the garden. Ideally, the stones should be big. The bigger, the better. Unfortunately, I have neither the strength nor the machinery to manage my dream boulders.

Instead, I use smaller stones, rubble, tiles, and mosaics in my projects. Here, you'll find several paving projects and mosaic projects, a compass rose in beach stone, and how to turn a slate tile into a pot with an edge.

In Bohuslän, on the west coast of Sweden, you can see ancient remnants of granite-quarrying.

A small detail from one of the large mosaics that adorn the walls in the Golden Hall at Stockholm City Hall. The Golden Hall contains more than 18 million mosaic tiles.

Stone has a breathtaking history, but when we say stone, we can be talking about many different types. There is marble, granite, slate, sandstone, gneiss, and many more types that have been created by nature over the course of several million years. And new stone is still continuing to be created. These all have their own unique structure and composition, and different stone varieties all have completely different traits.

In the past, stones were used to build walls that delineated land ownership and pastures; builders used the stones they found on the fields and in the wild.

Humans have been shaping stones since time immemorial. Building stone is the main product of the stone industry today, but stone is also used for grinding, in art, and in appliances.

From "Rock" to Stone

In quarries around the world, many different types of stones are mined and processed. Since ancient times, stonemasons have used hand tools to shape stones for paving and building.

Today, most rocks are shaped by machines with pneumatic tools. There is a big difference between the different rock types. Sandstone and limestone are relatively easy to work with, while granite and marble are significantly harder.

A Dry-Stacked Stone Wall Is a Piece of Art

A wall that is built without mortar or other joints is called a "dry-stacked stone wall." These are time-consuming to build, and you'll need both strength and patience. Each stone must be chosen with care not only to make the wall beautiful but also because the stones must fit together properly—otherwise, it won't be sturdy. This is an art that requires both talent and training. The end result is a beautiful wall that can withstand the passing of time and the forces of nature.

Stone Works

Stone works are as functional as they are beautiful, year after year.

Some people even think dry stone works become more beautiful with age when the stone has a little patina. As is the case with most things, the foundation is the key to a good result. By digging out the existing soil to a depth of 30–40 cm, you can fill the space with gravel to create the new foundation. To prevent the foundation from mixing with the subsoil, cover the soil with a ground cloth before laying the gravel. The foundation needs to be thoroughly vibrated so that it is properly compacted. Lastly, put a thin layer of sand or crushed stone as a base for the stones. In a walkway or pavement, the gaps between the stones should always be filled carefully, with paving sand for example. The joints are important for stabilizing the stones and keep the pavement stable.

Stone Mosaics

Mosaics are made from small pieces of colored stone that have been joined together to form an image or pattern. Up close, the pieces might seem random, but

In southern Europe, there are many examples of beautiful mosaics made of stones of contrasting colors. At the city gate of Ponta Delgada on São Miguel Island in the archipelago of Azores, black and white stones have been laid in a striking pattern.

At the Albrunna limestone quarry on Öland Island, birdwatchers intermingle with the active mining operations.

from a distance, the image becomes clear. Stone mosaics with figurative patterns decorated walls and flooring in Greece some 2500 years ago. The easiest way to make a mosaic is to make a mock-up. Draw the pattern on a piece of cardboard and place the tiles on it; this way, you can adjust the tiles until you're satisfied with how it looks. Leave enough space between each mosaic tile for the sealant. With square mosaic tiles, which are available in many colors, it's easy to create beautiful geometric patterns. If you want to create realistic motifs that require more detail, it's often better to use irregularly-shaped mosaic tiles in different color shades. You may need to shape the tiles with a wet saw so they fit the pattern.

The mosaic is created by gluing the bottoms of the tiles with an adhesive to the spot where they are to go. After the glue is dry, fill the gaps with a joint compound, remove any excess adhesive, and polish the stone surface.

Buy Stone with Caution

Today, you can buy the most common garden stones, such as small cobblestones, at the home improvement store. But there are also specialized stone companies that offer a wide range, and they can provide professional advice on materials and laying stone. If you want raw, natural stones or crushed stone, you can go to a gravel pit and load directly onto a trailer. Just remember that stone is heavy. Spare your spine, car, and trailer—do not load too much.

SAFETY

When you work with big stones, wearing steel-toed shoes is recommended. It's easy to pinch your foot when you're moving stones around.

• Wear rough work gloves to protect your hands from abrasions.

• Always wear a visor or goggles when you cut into stone. Shards often fly off and can cause serious eye damage. When grinding stone with an angle grinder, it's vital to use hearing protection to dull the high noise level.

• Use respiratory protection to protect your respiratory tract from the fine stone dust that is created when sawing stone.

In the Azores, you can admire the tall dry stone walls that make a part of the dreamy landscape. With their great skill, the builders have puzzled small stones together into beautiful walls.

A FLOWERBED FOR THE APPLE TREE

This big and beautiful Gravenstein apple tree is approximately eighty years old, and several of its big branches have died. Year after year the tree gives us gorgeous, early summer flowering of the most lovely shades, and the most juicy and delicious apples. We've made countless pies and cakes from these apples. Now that our younger trees have taken over the bulk of the apple production, this old tree has become a climbing support for a strong-growing climbing rose and a silk clematis. They cling to the tops of the bare branches and the tree crown is once again a sea of white flowers. A simple but stylish border of small cobblestones surrounds the new flowerbed we've made around the tree.

MATERIALS

- 1 string of 2.7 m
- 100 liters potting soil
- 50 liters cow manure
- 2.5 m² ground cloth
- 20 liters way sand
- 64 small cobblestones (10 x 10 x 10 cm)
- 4 rebars (each 2.5 m [10 mm])

TOOLS

- Scissors
- Spade
- Pitchfork
- Wheelbarrow
- Rubber mallet
- Bolt cutter

STEP BY STEP

A circular flowerbed with room for both fragrant vines and exciting lower perennials. Using a 2.7 m long string to measure, you can make a flower bed approximately 1.9 m in diameter.

1 Loop the string around the tree trunk and tie it. You will use this as a compass. Circle the trunk and use a spade to mark a trail in the grass. It's easiest if there are two of you so you can help each other. One can hold the string while and the other marks with the spade.

2 Peel off the layer of grass within the circle and loosen the soil with a pitchfork or large shovel.

3 Mix the cow manure and potting soil into the dirt.

4 The first plants can now be planted.

5 Dig a trench 15 cm deep around the outer edge of the flower bed.

6 Cover the trench with the ground cloth and fill with sand. Water the trench; step down on the sand to compress it. Place one of the cobblestones on top of the sand; confirm that the top of the cobblestone is level with the lawn. If it is not, add more sand.

7 Place the small cobblestones in the trench. They should stand close together. With a rubber mallet, knock the stones down into the sand so they are stable. Make sure all the stones are level with one other. Fill the gaps with sand.

8 Insert two rebars into the soil beside the climbing rose and two beside the silk clematis so they have something to climb on. The rebars should stand about 30 cm from the tree trunk. The rebars should be long enough to reach the tallest branches. Fasten the rebars to the branches with brackets so they stand steady.

SEA OF CLIMBING FLOWERS

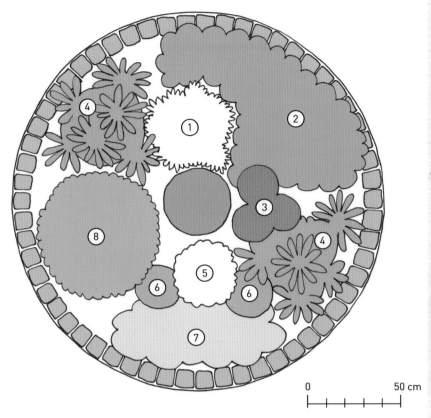

0   50 cm

1. Paul Farges
Clematis 'Summer
Snow'

2. Snake eye

3. Purple Coneflower
'Primadonna Deep
Rose'

4. Japanese Primrose
'Miller's Crimson'

5. Helen's Rose,
'Lykkefund'

6. Ashy Cranesbill
'Ballerina'

7. Spotted Dead
Nettle 'Pink Pewter'

8. Spring pea

Lamium maculatum

PLANTS

The flowerbed should be in a spot that is sunny most of the day. It will bloom from early spring all the way until autumn.

1. Paul Farges Clematis, *Clematis fargesioides* 'Summer Snow' (1 pc)
2. Snake eye, *verna* (3 pcs)
3. Purple Coneflower, *Echinacea purpurea*, 'Primadonna Deep Rose' (3 pcs)
4. Japanese primrose, *Primula japonica* 'Miller's Crimson' (10 pcs)
5. Helen's Rose, *Rosa helenae* 'Lykkefund' (1 pc)
6. Ashy Cranesbill, *Geranium cinereum* 'Ballerina' (2 pcs)
7. Spotted Dead Nettle, *Lamium maculatum* 'Pink Pewter' (1 pc)
8. Spring pea, *Lathyrus vernus* (1pc)

SLATE POT

Slate is a favorite material for the garden. The uneven, rough surfaces are possibly the most beautiful I've seen. The structure brings the slate alive and the gray colors play in the light. They can glisten in graphite gray or gleam silver, or be a discreetly livid blue-gray. I try to keep all my leftover pieces of slate and reuse them in new projects. I had a sheet of Offerdal slate left over after paving. What could it be used for? With the help of an angle grinder and some glue, the slate slab quickly metamorphosed into a modern and expressive pot. Ornamental grass provides a beautiful contrast to the rough stone surface.

MATERIALS

Makes a square pot that is 17 cm wide and 35 cm high.

- 1 piece of slate (13 x 350 x 780 mm)
- 1 wooden board (143 x 143 mm)
- stone glue for outdoor use
- 18 liters potting soil

TOOLS

- Angle grinder with cutting wheel suitable for stone
- Ruler
- Saw
- Drill
- Tile drill (6 mm)
- 2 m elastic cord
- Hammer
- Caulking gun to hold the glue

PLANTS

- Orange Sedge, *Carex testacea* 'Prairie Fire' (1 pc)

Many Colored Adhesives

There are glues and tile grouts in several colors. When gluing a slate pot, gray glue is more forgiving. Choose the shade that best matches your slate pieces.

STEP BY STEP

The slate I used was 35 x 78 cm and 13 mm thick. The pot size was chosen to make as little waste as possible. Ornamental grass softens the slate's elegant but slightly harsh appearance. 'Prairie Fire' turns a fiery orange color in autumn. It's quite fragile, so be sure to cover it in the fall or put it in the greenhouse during the winter, where it will be protected from the wind and extreme cold.

1 Cut the sidepieces and the pot base from the piece of slate. Use an angle grinder to cut the slate according to the spec drawing below. Also, cut the wooden board (143 x 143 mm); this will be used when gluing.

2 With a hammer, remove any protruding splinters from the cut wood. Then, drill an inch-wide drainage hole at the bottoms of two sidepieces. Wash off any dirt and stone dust from the slate.

3 Apply the stone glue to the surfaces that are to be placed together. I put masking tape near the edges, but this isn't necessary. Squeeze glue into the base's four edges. Then, apply glue along the long edges of the wider sidepieces.

4 Place the two wider sidepieces on the edges of the base, as shown in the image. Here, it's helpful to have a partner. One can hold the first two sidepieces and the other person can hold the other two.

5 Place the two narrower sidepieces on the base, between the wider sidepieces. Push the pieces together so the adhesive is distributed into the joints. Remove any excess glue.

6 Insert the wooden board into the pot opening and hold the pot together with the elastic cord. Let it stand for one day until the glue is dry.

Customize the Dimensions

Do you have a piece of slate with different dimensions than I listed here? It's easy to adjust the dimensions of the pot accordingly. The pot base should be square and two sidepieces should be as wide as the base is. The other two sidepieces should be as wide as the base plus two plate thicknesses. This way, the pot becomes a solid square when it's assembled.

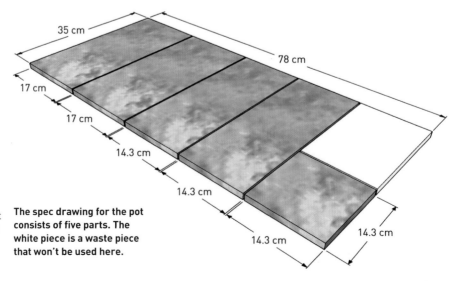

The spec drawing for the pot consists of five parts. The white piece is a waste piece that won't be used here.

35 cm
78 cm
17 cm
17 cm
14.3 cm
14.3 cm
14.3 cm
14.3 cm

RAISED FLOWER-BED OF BLASTED ROCK

MATERIALS

Makes an irregular flower bed of 3.4 x 1.8 m.
- 1 m³ quarried rock
- Flexible adhesive for outdoor use, e.g. Tremco PL 400
- 6 m² ground cloth
- 2 m³ potting soil

TOOLS

- 15 m of string
- Spade
- Glue gun
- Scissors

Heavy clay soil is nutrient-rich but is very compact and intractable. In order for the clay soil to become really good, a large amount of organic matter is required. When I was building a new perennial mini-garden, I wanted to avoid the backbreaking work of digging in the heavy clay, so instead I made a raised flowerbed. With dug-up rocks (or rip-rap) and stone glue, you can quickly put together a frame that can be filled with nutrient-rich, easily-to-handle soil. The jagged rocks give the flowerbed a tougher, wilder appearance than if it had been built with softer stones.

Aster divaricatus

STEP BY STEP

Places that sell sand and stone to individuals usually also have rip-rap. You can request to personally choose rocks that fit your flowerbed edge. Among the range of rip-rap is everything from rock dust to large boulders.

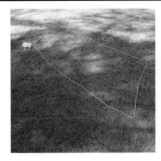

1 Arrange a string on the ground to mark the flowerbed's shape. Play with the shape until you are satisfied.

2 Wash the stones with the hose until most of the dust and dirt is rinsed off.

3 Peel off a groove of sod, approximately 30 cm wide.

4 Piece the rocks together to create a border. Secure any unstable rocks with glue. The border should be about 35 cm high.

5 Place a layer of newspaper along the inside of the flowerbed to prevent any weeds from growing through. Then, lay the ground cloth along the inside of the stone border; let the cloth pieces overlap by 10-20 cm. The cloth will prevent the soil from draining into the flowerbed.

6 Fill the raised bed with nutrient-rich potting soil, plant the flowers, and water thoroughly so the roots can make good contact with the earth.

Caring for Perennials

The raised flowerbed requires minimal maintenance and gives the perennials a good chance of surviving the winter. The plants soon grow together in the nutrient-rich and well-drained soil, and their thick roots prevent weeds from growing. Any weeds that find their way into the flowerbed are easy to remove.

Do not clean out the flowerbed in the autumn; leave the stems of the wilted perennials. Leaves and stems protect the plants during the winter. You can even intersperse dry autumn leaves between the plants to further improve their winter protection. In the spring, most of the leaves will have been taken care of by earthworms and have been turned into mulch. In the spring, once the first plants begin to show their new shoots, it will be time to clean out the flowerbed. Trim last year's stamens and compost them or remove the remaining dried leaves. Don't cut too close lest the new shoots be damaged. To fertilize, it's sufficient to cover the soil with a layer of cow manure 3–5 cm thick. I find it's practical to buy plastic bags of cow manure from the nursery. Fertilizer should be spread in the spring or early summer.

FIERY FROM SPRING TO FALL

1. Lungwort 'Sissing-hurst White'

2. Red-Veined Dock

3. White Wood Aster

4. Lady's Mantle

5. Coral Bells 'Plum Pudding'

6. Scarlet Beebalm

7. Mountain Fleece 'Firetail'

8. Hosta 'Stiletto'

9. Blue Fescue

10. Silver Mound 'Nana'

11. Purple Coneflower 'Starlight'

12. Turtlehead 'Alba'

13. Foxglove Beard-tongue 'Husker Red'

14. Red-Leafed Muk-denia 'Crimson Fans'

15. White Wood Violet 'Albiflora'

16. Leatherleaf Sedge

17. Lady Fern

18. Daylily 'Pardon Me'

19. Foam Flower 'Iron Butterfly'

20. Bugleweed

21. Windflower 'White Splendour'

22. Angel's Tears 'Thalia'

Early spring flowers
21. Windflower, *Anemone blanda*, 'White Splendour'
22. Angel's Tears, *Narcissus triandrus*, 'Thalia'

PLANTS

1. Lungwort, *Pulmonaria officinalis* 'Sissinghurst White' (4 pcs)
2. Red-Veined Dock, *Rumex sanguineus* (2 pcs)
3. White Wood Aster, *Eurybia divaricata* (1 pc)
4. Lady's Mantle, *Alchemilla mollis* (2 pcs)
5. Coral Bells, *Heuchera* 'Plum Pudding' (2 pcs)
6. Scarlet Beebalm, *Monarda didyma* (1 pc)
7. Mountain Fleece, *Bistorta amplexicaulis* 'Firetail' (1 pc)
8. Hosta, *Hosta* 'Stiletto' (6 pcs)
9. Blue Fescue, *Festuca glauca* (6 pcs)
10. Silver Mound, *Artemisia schmidtiana* 'Nana' (3 pcs)
11. Purple Coneflower, *Echinacea purpurea* 'Starlight' (9pcs)
12. Turtlehead, *Chelone obliqua* 'Alba' (1 pc)
13. Foxglove Beardtongue, *Penstemon digitalis* 'Husker Red' (1 pc)
14. Red-Leafed Mukdenia, *Mukdenia rossii* 'Crimson Fans' (1 pc)
15. White Wood Violet, *Viola sororia* 'Albiflora' (3 pcs)
16. Leatherleaf Sedge, *Carex buchananii* (1 pc)
17. Lady Fern, *Athyrium filix-femina* (1 pc)
18. Daylily, *Hemerocallis* 'Pardon Me' (1 pc)
19. Foam Flower, *Tiarella* 'Iron Butterfly' (3 pcs)
20. Bugleweed, *Ajuga reptans* (1 pc)

In a raised flowerbed the perennials get to thrive and be seen. 'Blood veined,' 'Bergamot,' and 'Starlight' compete for which can shine the most.

BEACH PEBBLE COMPASS ROSE

Orientation is important in a garden. Completely different plants thrive in the dark North than in the hot South. Having a compass in the garden may not be necessary, but to me, my compass is a gem. This compass rose is built from the red, green, and white stones I found on a beach in Montenegro. They have been polished by the waves and now feel soft and velvety. When wet, the stones shimmer like the most gorgeous gemstones. Let a stonemason engrave the cardinal directions in small cobblestones, and you can place them together with the compass rose before paving. The compass rose becomes an exquisite garden ornament that also guides you along your way.

MATERIALS

- 1 concrete slab (35 x 35 cm)
- 1 piece of plywood (35 x 35 cm)
- Approx. 2 liters beach stones of various colors
- Tile adhesive or mosaic concrete for outdoor use
- Tile joint filler for outdoor use

TOOLS

- Angle grinder, with cutting wheel suitable for stone
- Chisel
- Small sledgehammer
- Trowel
- Small bucket
- Notched trowel
- Joint filler
- Sponges
- Soft cloth

STEP BY STEP

This compass rose is just as beautiful in shades of black, gray, and white. However, the pattern becomes more prominent if you use complementary colors.

1 Draw a circle with a 35 cm diameter on a concrete slab. An easy way to do this is to use the rim of a bucket as a stencil, or see the tip on page 230. Make the same circle on the back of the slab.

2 Cut along the circle with an angle grinder. Flip the slab over and cut along the circle on that side, too.

3 Remove the corner pieces with a chisel and a small sledgehammer—if the pieces don't fall off by themselves. Trim off any sharp edges that stick out.

4 On the plywood board, draw a circle with a 35 cm diameter. Select stones that are pretty and even. Try out various placements of the stones to create a beautiful pattern for the concrete slab.

5 Mix the tile adhesive according to the instructions on the packaging and spread the adhesive on the concrete slab. With the notched trowel, even out the adhesive. The trowel's teeth will effectively spread the adhesive into a layer of moderate thickness.

6 Move the stone pattern from the plywood to the concrete. Start with the center stone and the outer edge stones. Fix the stones in the adhesive. Press lightly with a finger so the stones are set firmly in the adhesive.

7 When the compass rose is complete, gently wipe off any extra adhesive with a damp cloth. Let it stand level for two days so the adhesive dries properly.

8 Mix the tile joint filler according to the instructions on the packaging. Dollop the tile joint filler onto the compass rose. Work it into the gaps between the stones with a joint filler tool. Let it dry for about 10 minutes.

9 Wipe off the excess tile joint filler with a damp sponge. Rinse the sponge and wipe the stone surface several times until the surface is clean.

10 With a soft cloth, polish the stones and wipe off any remnants of the joint filler. The compass rose is now ready to be placed in the pavement.

TABLETOP FROM GRANDMA'S CHINA

MATERIALS

- 1 tin table (table top 60 cm in diameter)
- 15 porcelain plates with floral patterns
- 64 pieces of white glass mosaic (20 x 20 cm)
- 1 piece of plywood (60 x 60 cm)
- Tile adhesive or cement mosaic concrete for outdoor use
- Sealant for outdoor use

TOOLS

- Bolt cutter
- Mosaic pliers
- Trowel
- Small bucket
- Notched trowel
- Tile grout
- Sponges
- Soft cloth

When we cleaned out the cabinets in Grandma's kitchen, odd plates kept appearing—one right after the other. Some were chipped, on others the pattern had cracked. I took some of the most beautiful floral-patterned plates home with me to decorate a simple tin table. Sitting at the romantic mosaic table on a hot summer's day, freshly-made cinnamon buns and currant cordial taste especially wonderful. It brings back memories of childhood birthday parties in the garden, and I can still smell Grandma's baking in the air— though nearly half a century has passed since we ran around as children and played beside the sumptuously laid-out tables. If you don't have broken old china of your grandmother's or don't want to smash the intact pieces, there are plenty of lovely and inexpensive options for sale at flea markets, thrift shops, and yard sales.

STEP BY STEP

Tin tables are lightweight and have a flat surface that makes an ideal base for a mosaic. My tin table is 60 cm in diameter, and I bought it at a late summer sale. Just like with the china, it might be a good idea to look for tables at flea markets and thrift shops.

1 With a bolt cutter, cut the porcelain into large, rough pieces.

2 Cut these into small, irregular pieces and polish the jagged edges with mosaic pliers.

3 Trace the shape of the tabletop onto a sheet of plywood. Begin by laying out a border of white mosaic squares along the edge of the marked circle. The smooth edge will soften the appearance and will keep the mosaic pattern in place. Piece together the cut porcelain into a lovely mosaic.

4 Mix the tile adhesive following the instructions on the packaging. Start by spreading the adhesive around the outer edge of the table top. Don't spread too much; you'll have to place the porcelain pieces quickly before the adhesive dries—in approximately 15 minutes.

5 Spread the adhesive with a notched trowel. The teeth spread the adhesive quickly and effectively. Start with the border of white mosaic squares; place them on the adhesive. Lightly press the squares with your finger so the pieces are set firmly in the adhesive.

6 Place the porcelain pieces, one by one, onto the adhesive. It's a good idea to move from the outside in, so place the pieces that abut the border first.

7 Add more adhesive as you go, and continue to distribute the adhesive with the notched trowel. When the border is done, set the center pieces in place on the adhesive. Then proceed with the rest of the surface until the mosaic is complete. With a soft cloth, gently wipe off any excess adhesive.

8 Mix the joint filler following the instructions on the packaging and dollop it onto the tabletop. Wipe the adhesive over the porcelain with a joint filler tool; work the joint filler into the gaps. Let it dry for about 10 minutes.

9 Wipe off any excess joint filler with a wet sponge. Rinse the sponge in clean water and wipe the table surface several times until all excess joint filler is gone.

10 Polish the tabletop with a soft cloth. The table is now ready to use.

PERSONALIZED WALKWAY

The garden path takes us to different places amongst the flowers. It connects the various components of the garden, and gives us a surface to step upon that doesn't damage the plants. Through the choice of material and shape, you can give the walkway the appearance and expressiveness that best reflects you. Let the character of your house, as well as its age inspire you. A winding narrow path through the grove or stepping stones on the lawn look light and airy. A wide walkway gives a more solid and stable impression. A walkway made of concrete slabs is practical and easy to maintain, and if you combine the standard-sized, store-bought slabs with personalized slabs you've made yourself, the walkway will be unique and beautiful to look at (see page 63). This walkway is built according to two interesting number sequences; read more about them on the following page.

MATERIALS

Makes a 10 m-long walkway.

- 10 m² ground cloth
- 1 m³ of gravel for the foundation layer (⁰⁄₃₂)
- 0.25 m³ sand or rock dust (⁰⁄₄ or ⁰⁄₈)
- 17 store-bought concrete slabs (5 x 35 x 35 cm)
- 9 personalized concrete slabs (see p 63)
- 5 concrete blocks on mesh, e.g. Strong Carpet Stone (1200 x 400 x 40 mm)
- 37 kg jointing sand
- 10 m planks to support an edge when jointing (20 m if support is needed for both sides)
- 4 m² protective plastic film

TOOLS

- Ruler
- Spade
- Rake
- Spirit level
- Soil compactor
- Rubber mallet
- Scissors
- Broom
- Hose

STEP BY STEP

This walkway consists of a single row of standard, store-bought slabs interspersed with personalized slabs that have unique patterns. The row is framed by 9 x 9 cm concrete blocks that are similar to small cobblestones in their shape; however, they are much easier to put down because they are of uniform thickness. Cut strips from the mesh and the installation will be easy.

1 Remove 25 cm of dirt where the walkway is to be constructed. Cover the soil with a ground cloth and distribute the gravel evenly over the surface. Either vibrate the gravel with a soil compactor or step down on the gravel to create a smooth, hard surface.

2 On the gravel surface, rake out a layer of jointing sand or rock dust to be 4 cm thick. Compress the sand; the surface should be hard and flat. The bottom of the slabs will stand on the surface, so make sure the height of the sand surface is as you want it.

3 Use a spirit level to confirm that the surface is flat. Place the slabs and the concrete blocks where the walkway is to begin (see the illustration on the bottom of the next page for the proper order in which the slabs should be laid down). Start with the concrete slabs; put a row of blocks between each slab. Knock the slabs down into the sand with a rubber mallet so they are flat, stable, and level.

4 Check regularly as you go to ensure that the slabs are level. Finish the slab section by laying the border of concrete blocks along the walkway. I placed my walkway beside a high steel rim that runs along the hedges. Place the concrete blocks so there is a smooth gap of equal width around all the slabs. Knock the blocks down into the sand until they stand at the same level as the slabs. You may need to top up with some sand.

5 Finish laying down the slabs and blocks of the walkway.

6 Place plastic film around the planks and place them so they support the walkway's outer edge. The planks will help to create a stylish, durable, and even outer edge. Distribute sand over the dry, freshly installed walkway. Use a broom to fill the gaps with jointing sand. Be sure to remove any excess jointing sand.

7 Spray water over the walkway for about 10–15 seconds. Allow it to dry for 5 minutes. Then spray the walkway with water again, until the joints are completely saturated.

8 After approximately one day, the joint sand will have hardened and formed stiff joints that neither weeds nor ants will be able to break through.

The Curiosities of Number Sequences

Fibonacci was an Italian mathematician who lived during the thirteenth century. His number sequence has remarkable properties, and it appears constantly in nature and art. When new leaves grow from the stem of a plant, they usually grow in a spiral. The spiral twists as it climbs upward. Nature distributes leaves in a special way—entirely according to the Fibonacci sequence.

After five laps, eight leaves sprout. After eight laps, thirteen leaves sprout. Could it be that nature distributes leaves in this manner to prevent the upper leaves from casting the lower ones into too much shadow?

Seeds in pinecones lie hidden beneath the pinecone's scales. The scales are also arranged according to the Fibonacci sequence—in spirals around the cone. When you count the number of spiral arcs that go clockwise and the number of spiral arcs that go counterclockwise, you will discover that these are two consecutive Fibonacci numbers.

The Fibonacci sequence starts with 0 and 1. Every number thereafter is then the sum of the two previous numbers, that is, 0, 1, 1, 2, 3, 5, 8, 13, 21, 34, 55, 89, 144, etc.

Prime numbers are integers that are bigger than 1 and that can only be evenly divided by itself and 1. These are 2, 3, 5, 7, 11, 13 17, 19, 23, 29, 31, 37, etc.

The seeds in sunflower seedpods form clockwise and counterclockwise spirals. I counted 55 and 89 spiral arcs on my sunflower.

The small disk flowers in *Echinacea purpurea* 'Starlight' are arranged in 21 left-handed spiral arcs and 34 right-handed.

The number of spiral arcs that the scales form to the right and to the left are both Fibonacci numbers. The great American pinecone has 13 and 21 spiral arcs. The small Swedish alder cone, larch cone, and pinecone from the Azores all have 5 and 8 spiral arcs.

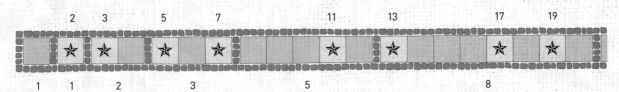

Walkway Design

I used two mathematical number sequences as the starting point for my walkway. I was inspired by prime numbers and the Fibonacci sequence. The upper number sequence is composed of prime numbers. These mark the locations of the personalized concrete slabs I made by hand.

The lower number sequence is the number of concrete slabs between the transverse rows of pebbles. They've been selected in accordance with the Fibonacci sequence.

CHAPTER Nº 25

STONE AND BRICKLAYING

Layers

Applying mortar is almost like baking cake. The mortar is used to bind bricks, and you make the "cake" layer by layer. I love walls and think they're one of the most decorative elements a garden can have. The most beautiful walls are made of natural stone or old brick. In this chapter, the small steps and stone pedestal are quick projects. The ruined wall and the lion's head fountain are big projects that take a little longer, but, when completed, will give the garden a lovely ambiance.

The front of a large manor house in Tavistock in Devon, England. Nature is beginning to reclaim the remains of an old stone wall.

Masonry is a traditional skill that hasn't much changed since the days of our ancestors. Today, just like in the past, we bind units of natural stone and brick together with mortar. To make large churches and houses through masonry requires huge amounts of skill and is a professional job. However, most of us have the know-how to make smaller walls for our gardens.

Laying Stone

Natural stones such as granite, diabase, and limestone are mined in large quarries and cut into building blocks. Because they vary in size, structure, and color, great skill is required to mortar natural stone. However, there are few materials that make bridges, basements, and walls as comparably beautiful and solid as stone can.

Brick—An Artificial Building Stone

Brick consists mainly of dried or baked clay. Hand-cut brick is, as the name suggests, made by hand and shaped with wooden molds. Machine-made bricks are shaped by roller presses.

Today, there are only a few isolated brickworks left in Sweden, and most bricks are imported. In the past, some bricks were stamped with the brickyard's name or crest, so you could see where the bricks were manufactured. When I built my romantic ruin, I used old bricks (see page 163). I found some bricks that had been stamped for quality-control, but none had brickyard stamps.

The cheapest type of brick is the masonry brick. It's used for hidden masonry structures, such as walls that will be polished or suspended.

There are also frost resistant bricks and refractory bricks.

Facing brick is used, as its name states, for building facings.

In addition to different varieties and qualities of brick, brick also comes in different sizes. The dimensions of bricks have varied over the centuries, and today they vary from country to country.

Standard brick size in Sweden is 250 mm long, 120 mm wide and 62 mm high. Bricks are usually 4:2:1 in length, width, and thickness. This way, stones placed in different directions can be cemented together into different types of bonds. Bricks with underlying bonds are called a shift.

The simplest wall bond is the running bond and Flemish bond. A running bond is when each shift consists of bricks lying along the wall's length.

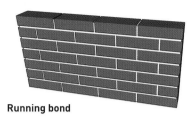

Running bond

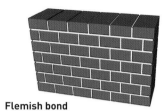

Flemish bond

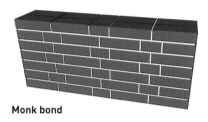

Monk bond

In the running bond and Flemish bond, bricks lie along the wall (stretchers) and are perpendicular to the wall (headers). A monk bond consists of stretchers and headers. If the shifts are laid unevenly, it will give the wall a different character.

Combining natural stone and brick can make an eye-catching effect. This little house in Mevagissey in Cornwall has a facade of natural stone masonry, and the gate is beautifully framed by brick.

TOP: Sweden's 17th century Brahehus Castle is primarily natural stone masonry. Today, the windows still open to delicious panoramic views of Visingsö and Lake Vättern.
BOTTOM: Some of the bricks in my wall have pretty stamps.

I used a running bond for the ruined wall.

If the stones are laid the opposite ways at a 45° angle to the direction of the wall, this is called a header.

Other examples of bonds are the monk, cross, block, Dutch, American, and English bonds.

The Mortar Bonds

The mortar that bonds bricks together forms a joint that can smooth out both the imperfections of the bricks and pressure from overlying bricks.

The mortar usually consists of limestone or concrete, and fine sand mixed with water. Dry premix can be purchased in eighty-pound bags. Follow the mixing instructions on the packaging. To keep a wall from cracking, it will need to have a solid foundation. A piece cast in concrete should reach frost-free depth. If you are building a long wall, it may be necessary to support the wall with columns at each end and evenly distributed supports.

Time for Shopping

Masonry, bricks, and mortar are available in home improvement stores. Bring gloves to the store if you don't need entire pallets-worth of building materials. They'll be useful when loading.

Different kinds of mortar are suitable for different uses. Consult the staff in the store to find out which product best suits your purposes. Keep the bags of mortar dry to prevent the mortar from curing prematurely.

SAFETY

It's vital that you use both gloves and a respirator when mixing the mortar. The limestone in the mortar dries out your skin and will irritate your respiratory tract.

• Protect your hands and feet with heavy-duty gloves and steel-toed boots.

• Protect your eyes with safety-glasses or a face shield or glasses when chopping stone or brick. Shards will often fly off and can cause serious eye damage.

• Wear hearing protection to guard against the high noise level when cutting brick or stone. Wear a respirator to protect against the fine brick and stone dust.

SMALL STONE STEPS

A flat garden certainly has its advantages. A level surface is good for playing games and for positioning terraces and sun decks. It's also much easier to steer the wheelbarrow laden with potting soil or stones around the garden. That being said, a flat garden may look and feel boring. Adding levels will make your garden more exciting and interesting; you can add a small mound with shrubs or a sunken surface paved with stones for garden furniture. Small decorative stone steps in our garden link the pathway to the greenhouse and accentuate an 20 cm difference in the level of the ground.

MATERIALS

- 2m² ground cloth
- 80 liters crushed rock ($^0/_{12}$)
- 18 large pavement stones (10 x 14 x 20 cm)
- 20 liters rock flour ($^0/_4$)
- 25 kg concrete
- 40 liters red porphyry gravel ($^8/_{11}$)

GEAR

- Yardstick or tape measure
- Spade
- Scissors
- Spirit level
- Angle grinder with stone cutting wheel
- Chisel
- Hammer
- Bucket
- Trowel

Cutting Large Paving Stones

Make an incision with an angle grinder where the stone needs to be cut. Here is the corner that should be removed.

Insert a chisel into the cut and lightly tap the chisel with a hammer.

The cuts do not need to be deeper than this to divide the stone nicely.

STEP BY STEP

Because our walkway was elevated 20 cm above its surroundings, two shallow steps with a height of 10 cm were needed. The steps were 40 cm deep and 60 cm wide, and filled with porphyry aggregate, just like the existing walkway. Start by digging away 15 cm of soil where the stairs are to be constructed.

1 Cover the excavation with a ground cloth. Fill it up with crushed rock. Compress the crushed rock layer by watering it and treading on it. You can use a soil compactor to compress the substrate if you're making larger steps.

2 Place the first layer of large paving stones, which will become the base for the two steps (see drawing below). Check the stones with a spirit level. Trim any corners from the stones that will come in contact with the existing pavement (see previous page).

3 Mix the concrete according to the instructions on the packaging. Bond the large paving stones with concrete. Allow the concrete to cure for 3–4 hours before you start on the next layer.

4 Cut 3 paving stones vertically. They will form the raised lip on the upper step. Position the halved stones and bond them together with concrete.

5 Fill the bottom of the two steps with stone dust. Compress the stone dust to a hard, flat surface. Cover the surface with a ground cloth.

6 Lastly, fill the steps with the red porphyry gravel.

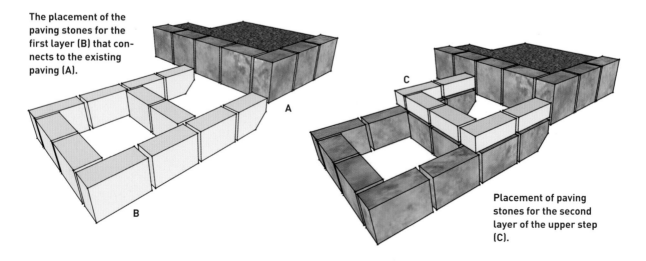

The placement of the paving stones for the first layer (B) that connects to the existing paving (A).

A

B

C

Placement of paving stones for the second layer of the upper step (C).

STONE PEDESTAL

Do you have any garden decorations that you're especially fond of? I have an urn from Greece that I wanted to highlight, so now it stands on a stone pedestal. The urn isn't perfectly round, and the ears are a bit uneven, but that's what makes it so charming. The style is called Pithos and it comes from Volyrakis pottery, in Crete, where they have manufactured ceramics by hand for generations. The Mediterranean vibe is enhanced by the fragrant lavender that surrounds the stone pedestal.

MATERIALS

- 2.5 m batten (25 x 120 mm)
- 50 cm triangular rod (50 x 50 mm)
- 4 brackets (90°)
- 8 wood screws (4 x 30 mm)
- 1 m² ground cloth
- 5 crusher buckets each containing 20 liters (⅛ and ⁹⁄₁₂)
- 87.5 kg rough concrete
- 3 m rebar (8 mm)
- 1 piece of protective plastic (1 x 1 m)
- 50–75 kg concrete
- 1 m² raw trimmed slate
- 1 slate plate (30 x 30 cm)
- 2 buckets of filling, such as brick and stone

FOR PLANTING SURFACE

- 2m² ground cloth
- 48 small cobblestones (10 x 10 x 10 cm)
- 40 liters rock dust
- 100 liters of sand mixed with potting soil

TOOLS

- Ruler
- Saw
- Screwdriver
- Bolt cutter
- Marking sticks
- Spade
- Scissors
- Spirit level
- Concrete mixing paddle or cement mixer
- Bucket and trowel
- String line
- Shovel
- Rubber mallet

STEP BY STEP

Make sure you have a circle of free space that is 1.6 m in diameter around the stone pedestal. This is where you will build a flowerbed. Build the casting frame for the base slab and mark the area where it is to be placed.

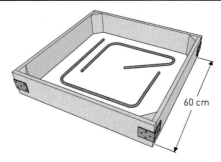

Cut the boards into two pieces that are 60 cm and 2 pieces that are 65 cm. Cut a triangular rod into four pieces. The pieces should sit on the inner corners for support. Assemble the frame with angle brackets on the outside. Cut the rebars and bend them according to the diagram so that the pieces will fit in the frame. They should be placed 5–10 cm away from the frame's inner edge.

1 Dig a ditch that is 30 cm deep. Cover the bottom and walls of the ditch with a ground cloth. Fill it with crushed stones to ground level. Compress the gravel by watering it and treading on it. Level the surface and confirm it is straight with a spirit level. Place the frame for the slab on the compacted gravel's surface.

2 Mix the coarse concrete according to the instructions on the packaging. Pour the concrete into the mold until it is half-full. Place the bent rebar onto the surface of the concrete for reinforcement.

3 Fill the mold the rest of the way with concrete. Tap the outside of the mold with the rubber mallet and pump a rebar up and down in the wet concrete to remove the air bubbles. Level the concrete surface by shearing off excess concrete with the edge of a wooden beam.

4 Cover the frame with plastic sheeting and let the concrete cure for about 3 days. During this time, occasionally remove the plastic and spray the concrete with water. When the concrete has finished curing, remove the mold. If it's stuck to the concrete, unscrew the brackets and remove each plank separately.

5 Mix the concrete according to the instructions on the bag. Make the stone pedestal a little smaller than the base slab (see the drawing on the next page). Place the border stones on the first layer and bond them. Add filler and fill the gaps with concrete. Allow the concrete to cure for 1–2 hours.

6 Mark the stone pedestal's height with string. Check with a spirit level to ensure that the horizontal strings are straight. Continue to lay brick on brick so that the outer edges and upper edge of the pedestal are as flat as possible. Fill up the inside of the stone pedestal with stone, brick, and concrete.

7 Finish by bonding a square slate slab on the top of the pedestal. Check with a spirit level to confirm that the slab is level.

8 The slate slab makes a simple, classic base for the urn. The pedestal is now done and it's time to make the flower bed and to plant the plants.

1 Mark a circle around the pedestal with a 1.6-m diameter (see page 230). Remove the sod. Loosen the soil with a pitchfork.

2 Dig a 15 cm-deep gutter at the edge of the flower bed. Place a ground cloth at the bottom. Fill it with stone dust and tread on the surface. Place the small paving stones and adjust their height by adding or removing stone dust.

3 Hammer the stones down into the stone dust so that the top of the stone is level with the surrounding lawn. Load in the potting soil. Make sure the pedestal base slab is covered and that the earth's surface descends toward the stone edge.

4 For my flower bed I used 16 lavender plants— *Lavandula angustifolia* 'Hidcote Blue.' In early July, the buds will blossom abundantly, and will continue to do so throughout the month. With luck, you'll still be getting new flowers even at the end of the summer.

5 Fill the gap between the stone edge and the surrounding lawn with stone dust. Water the lavender plants thoroughly before planting them along the border.

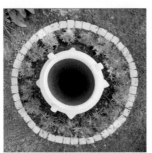

6 Distribute the plants evenly around the pedestal. Water the plants until they establish themselves on the plant site. Lavender is a very drought-tolerant plant, and therefore doesn't need to be watered at all.

The Baseboard Should Be Bigger

Build the stone pedestal's edges 5 cm into the bottom slab's perimeter. Try to find slate stones that have a relatively smooth edge. Piece the stones together so the edges of the pedestal and the top are as smooth as possible.

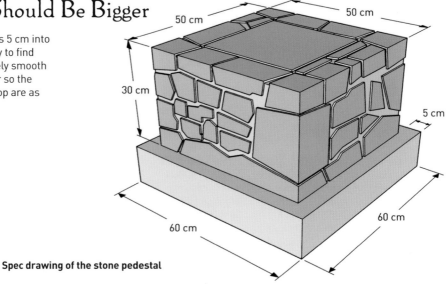

50 cm · 50 cm · 30 cm · 5 cm · 60 cm · 60 cm

Spec drawing of the stone pedestal

Butterflies love to visit lavender. Here is a cabbage butterfly that has landed on a 'Hidcote Blue.'

That Heavenly Fragrance

Touch a lavender plant gently and it will spread a wonderful fragrance that is attractive to both humans and butterflies. It's soothing to watch butterflies flit from flower to flower.

Lavender, *Lavandula angustifolia*, is a perennial small shrub. The flowers hover over the gray-green or silver-gray foliage of their long stems. The blooms often range among shades of blue-violet, but there are also pink and white variations. 'Hidcote Blue' has blue-violet flowers, 'Artic Snow' blooms in white, and 'Rosea' in pink.

Plant the lavender in a dry and sunny place. It does not like moisture. One of the toughest lavender varieties is the violet blooming 'Munstead.'

During the spring, when the lavender starts to grow new shoots, it should be pruned to maintain a pretty appearance. Cut it down, but do not remove the bottom shoots. It can sometimes be difficult to break new shoots in the woody strain.

I usually keep the cut shoots and grow new lavender plants. Crop the shoots to about 7 cm and shave off the leaves from the stem. There should only be a small rosette of leaves at the top. Put 5–6 shoots together in a bunch and stick the stems directly into sandy soil, all the way down to the leaf rosette. Water them so that they don't dry out, and they will soon form roots. If you put them in rows and keep a 6-inch distance between the bunches, you'll have the beginning of a new lavender hedge.

In the Middle Ages, lavender was used as perfume and medicine. It's considered to be an analgesic, as well as an antiseptic, expectorant, and anticonvulsant.

Today, lavender is cultivated on a large scale in the Mediterranean for the perfume and cosmetics industries. You can also spice meat with lavender leaves and use the flowers in baked goods. Some insects shun the fragrance of lavender, so lavender can also be used as mothballs. Dry the lavender flowers and put them in a small linen bag; put this in the closet to protect your textiles and keep them smelling fresh and fragrant.

WETLAND

Many of us dream of a lush garden, but in order for this to happen, your plants have to thrive. The right soil, light, and water conditions are crucial. Near big trees, the soil is often bone dry and the earth is invaded with roots. In this case, it makes little sense to plant the plants in native soil. Your solution can be a wetland that is either an elevated or lowered cultivation bed with integrated reservoirs. Plants that are not drought-resistant will thrive in a wetland. I built mine out of natural stone. A wetland is perfect for those who want lush perennials that require minimal maintenance.

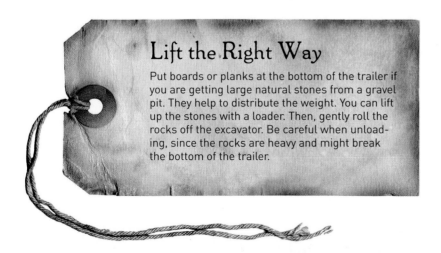

Lift the Right Way

Put boards or planks at the bottom of the trailer if you are getting large natural stones from a gravel pit. They help to distribute the weight. You can lift up the stones with a loader. Then, gently roll the rocks off the excavator. Be careful when unloading, since the rocks are heavy and might break the bottom of the trailer.

MATERIALS

Makes a 50 cm high wetland surrounded by 10 m stone edge.

- 6 buckets crushed rock 20 liters each (⁰⁄₁₆)
- 12 m² ground cloth
- 1 m³ of natural stone (10–40 cm)
- 150 kg cement
- 1 dust cloth or thick tarpaulin (2.1 x 4.2 m)
- 1 m³ skeletal material such as large rocks or aerated concrete pieces
- 1 tube of hard plastic at 30 cm (5 cm in diameter)
- 1 piece of fine-mesh wire (10 x 10 cm)
- 2 cable ties
- 1 m drain hose (80 mm inside diameter)
- 1 end plug (DN80)
- 3 m³ potting soil

TOOLS

- 6 marking pegs
- Yardstick or tape measure
- Spade
- Mini excavator (suggested; this is available for rent)
- Spirit level
- Rake
- Pruning shears
- Wheelbarrow
- Scissors
- Concrete mixer
- Bucket
- Trowel
- Shovel
- String line
- Hacksaw

STEP BY STEP

Choose a location where the bottom of the wetland can be completely flat, and mark its shape on the ground. If you are building a wetland of a different shape, calculate the linear feet of stone edge and the materials you need. It takes about 150 kg of stone and 8 liters of concrete to make a linear stone edge. Try to get a hold of rocks of assorted sizes to bring your wall to life.

1 Remove any sod, roots, and rocks. It might be easier to rent a small excavator for the heavy work. If you can dig out enough of the soil that the ground level is lowered, then the wall doesn't need to be very high. The key is to make the wetland about 50 cm deep.

2 Clear any remaining roots and pebbles by hand. Rake the surface and check with a spirit level to make sure it is flat.

3 Dig a 25 cm-wide and 5 cm-deep trench along the edge of the wetland and cover the trench with a ground cloth. Fill it with crushed rock and compress the gravel by stepping on it.

4 Place the largest blocks down as the first layer. Align the stones as needed so they fit together to create an even outer edge. Stabilize the bigger stones by wedging in smaller rocks on the inside of the wall.

5 Mix the concrete by following the instructions on the bag. Continue to piece together the stones and bond them with concrete. If necessary, you can also create flat surfaces with concrete to create a solid foundation for the next layer of stones.

6 When the wall is 15 cm high at the lowest point, it's time to begin work on the water reservoir. If you have any extra mixed concrete left in the bucket, find some way to use it before beginning the next step.

7 Place a thick ground cloth or tarp in the wetland. It should be large enough to reach up at least 25 cm along the wetland's inner wall. Once, I used a thick yellow tarp that my neighbor was about to throw out.

8 Press the tarp down into the ground and onto the inner wall. Trim off any excess tarp.

9 To create a space for the water reservoir, you need a 15 cm-thick skeleton base. Large voids will form between the skeleton stones, which will fill with the water that creates the wetland's waterbed. My neighbor was building a garage, so I managed to use his building remnants of concrete and lightweight aggregate blocks.

10 For the water reservoir, an outlet pipe is needed to direct out excess water. Attach a dense wire with cable ties around the opening. Place the outlet pipe so that it rests on the skeleton layer's top edge, and goes through the wetland's wall, between the stones. It should slope downward slightly.

11 Place the drain hose on the opposite side of the outlet pipe. Put the hose at the bottom of the water reservoir. It should extend to the top of the wall. Fresh water will fill the reservoir through this pipe.

12 Cover the skeleton layer with ground cloth. Only the outlet and filling pipe should stick out from the cloth. The reservoir is now done.

13 Mix the fresh concrete and continue to build the stone wall by piecing it together, layer by layer. When you are approaching the designated height, you will need strings.

14 Hammer down marker sticks outside each corner. Clamp the wall strings between the bars so that they are in line with the top of the wall. Check with a spirit level to confirm that the string and the top of the wall are level.

15 Now it is time to fill the wetland with nutritious earth. I mix sandy potting soil with compost soil for my plants.

16 Fill the water tank through the filling tube. The wetland is ready for planting.

17 Cut away excess filling tube just above ground level by the wall's upper edge.

18 Put a cap on the filling tube to prevent small animals and debris from falling in.

19 Place the plants on the bed and adjust the position of each plant until you are satisfied.

20 Plant the plants in the bed. Water them so the roots make good contact with the earth. If rainfall has been poor during the summer, you'll need to fill the reservoir a few times.

GROWING IN THE PENUMBRA

1. Creeping Jenny 'Goldilocks'

2. Hosta 'Golden Waffles'

3. Scaly Male Fern 'Crispa Gracilis'

4. Chinese Silver Grass 'Kleine Fontaine'

5. Hard Fern

6. Hard Shield Fern

7. Chinese Silver Grass 'Kleine Silberspinne'

8. Coral Bells 'Lime Rickey'

9. Drumstick Primrose

10. Geranium Rozanne 'Gerwat'

11. Giant Hyssop 'Black Adder'

12. Hyssop

13. Hakone Grass 'Aureola'

14. Purple Cranesbill

15. Pendulous Bellflower

16. Speedwell 'Knallblau'

17. Japanese Aster 'Starshine'

18. Black Mondo Grass

19. Iceland Poppy 'Pacino'

20. Hakone Grass 'All Gold'

21. Woodland Crocus 'Barr's Purple'

22. Flowering Onion 'Purple Sensation'

Spring onion

Planted in groups between the perennials.
21. *Crocus tommasinianus* 'Barr's Purple'
22. *Allium hollandicum* 'Purple Sensation'

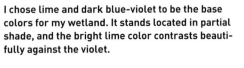

I chose lime and dark blue-violet to be the base colors for my wetland. It stands located in partial shade, and the bright lime color contrasts beautifully against the violet.

PLANTS

1. *Creeping Jenny, Lysimachia nummularia* 'Goldilocks' (10 pcs)
2. Hosta, *Hosta* 'Golden Waffles' (1pc)
3. Scaly Male Fern, *Dryopteris affinis* 'Crispa Gracilis' (1 pc)
4. Chinese Silver Grass, *Miscanthus sinensis* 'Kleine Fontaine' (1 pc)
5. Hard Fern, *Blechnum spicant* (3 pcs)
6. Hard Shield Fern, *Polystichum aculeatum* (1 pc)
7. Chinese Silver Grass, *Miscanthus sinensis* 'Kleine Silberspinne' (1 pc)
8. Coral Bells, *Heuchera* 'Lime Rickey' (6 pcs)
9. Drumstick Primrose, *Primula denticulata* (3 pcs)
10. Geranium Rozanne 'Gerwat' (1 pc)
11. Giant Hyssop, *Agastache* 'Black Adder' (3 pcs)
12. Hyssop, *Hyssopus officinalis* (12 pcs)
13. Hakone Grass, *Hakonechloa macra* 'Aureola' (1 pc)
14. Purple Cranesbill, *Geranium x magnificum* (1 pc)
15. Pendulous Bellflower, *Campanula pendula* (5 pcs)
16. Speedwell, *Veronica austriaca* 'Knallblau' (3 pcs)
17. Japanese Aster, *Aster ageratoides* 'Starshine' (1 pc)
18. Black Mondo Grass, *Ophiopogon planiscapus* 'Nigrescens' (5 pcs)
19. Iceland Poppy, *Papaver miyabeanum* 'Pacino' (3 pcs)
20. Hakone Grass, *Hakonechloa macra* 'All Gold' (3 pcs)

0   50 cm

LION'S HEAD FOUNTAIN

There are many like myself who have dull, empty corners in the garden. Our lifeless corner was situated by the driveway and was very noticeable. There was a rocky slope facing south that had no beautiful plants, and a trash can was the only focal point. After reading a number of books on Italian and English gardens, I was inspired to build a fountain. Today, our stone lion peeks out from under the big oak tree and welcomes us with the happy sound of trickling water. The trash can is now hidden behind a narrow carpinus hedge, and our corner has been transformed from a weed-shrouded slope to a tranquil spot with splashes of the Mediterranean.

Mortar with Irregular Stone

Making a wall out of irregular Oppdal slate is like piecing together a jigsaw puzzle. Spread out the slate pieces on a flat surface so it's easier to find the right piece for your project.

MATERIALS

BASE MATERIALS
- 1 bendable Flexible MDF (9 x 1220 x 2440 mm)
- 1 particle board (12 x 1200 x 2500 mm)
- 1 box of nails (35 x 1.7 mm)

THE LION'S BACK PIECE
- Approx. 30 small nails (25 mm)
- 30 cm plastic tube 1"
- 4 sticks 40 cm (10 mm)
- 2 m cord
- Duct tape
- 2 L-hooks (50 mm)
- 25 kg concrete

THE MOLDS AND REINFORCEMENT
- 6 m stud (22 x 120 mm)
- 2 m battens (25 x 38 mm)
- 20 m rebar (8 mm)

THE GROUND AND THE FOUNTAIN
- Wheat flour for marking
- 4 m² ground cloth
- 0.25 m² gravel (⁹/₃₂)
- 400 kg coarse concrete
- 1 piece of plastic (2 x 2.5 m)
- 25 cm plastic tube 1"
- 14 large pavement stones
- 150 kg mortar
- 2 m² crude carved Oppdal slate
- 36 small pavement stones
- 1 piece of plywood (1.2 x 1.3 m)
- Duct tape and plastic sheeting
- 2 solid slate tiles (25 x 600 x 350 mm)
- 1 lion's head
- Silicone
- One adjustable fountain pump
- 2 m garden hose ½"

TOOLS

- Ruler
- Saw
- Hammer
- Drill driver
- Drill bit (30 mm)
- Scissors
- Concrete mixer or concrete mixing paddle
- Bucket
- Trowel
- Bolt cutter
- Spade
- Spirit level
- Angle grinder with stone cutting wheel
- Chisel
- Small sledgehammer

STEP BY STEP

Building a lion's head fountain is a pretty major undertaking. I did it at a leisurely pace during the summer, and it took several months. Plan for at least two weeks. Stone lion's heads are available at well-stocked garden centers, Oppdal slate at stone companies, and the other supplies can be found at home improvement stores. Start by sawing the MDF and particle board. Be sure to draw out all parts before you begin cutting. Then, build three molds. First, prepare the shape of the oval backing, which is needed to support the lion's head against the fountain wall's irregular slate stones. Then, make the molds for the ground and the water reservoir.

[Cut spec for the grooved MDF]

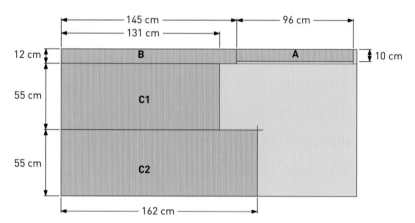

Draw all the parts that are to be cut out from the MDF. If you have another shape for a fountain or a different lion's head than what I show here, it's important to adapt the sizes of the pieces to your fountain in your drawing. The pieces must be placed so that they can fit. The gray surface becomes waste.

[Cut spec for the particle board]

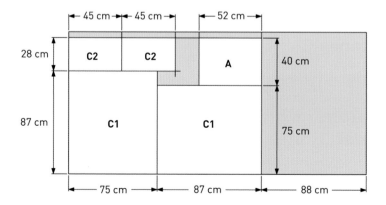

Draw the parts on the particle board. Double-check all measurements before cutting. Make sure to check the dimensions of piece A if you need to adapt it to a lion's head that is different from the one I used. The gray surface becomes waste.

[Lion's head cover]

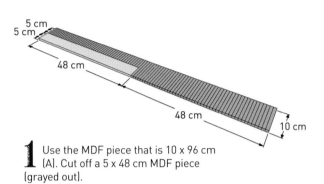

5 cm
5 cm
48 cm
48 cm
10 cm

1 Use the MDF piece that is 10 x 96 cm (A). Cut off a 5 x 48 cm MDF piece (grayed out).

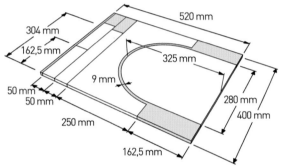

520 mm
304 mm
162,5 mm
325 mm
9 mm
50 mm
50 mm
280 mm
400 mm
250 mm
162,5 mm

2 Use the particle board piece that is 40 x 52 cm (A). Draw an ellipse (see next page) that is 32.5 cm along the major axis and 28 cm along the minor axis. Make the loop on the string 24.5 cm, with the distance between the foci 16.5 cm. Continue drawing all the pieces that are to be cut out from the particle board. The narrow oval strip that runs around the edge of the ellipse is 9 mm wide. It is easily done by measuring the distance outward from the ellipse line with a ruler, and marking a new line with a pencil. Cut out all parts with a saw and put them aside. The gray bits become waste.

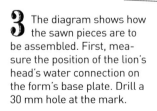

3 The diagram shows how the sawn pieces are to be assembled. First, measure the position of the lion's head's water connection on the form's base plate. Drill a 30 mm hole at the mark.

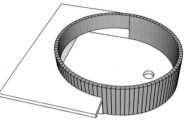

4 Nail the pieces together according to the diagram.

5 Insert the 30 cm-long plastic tubing through the hole and seal inwardly as shown in the image. Secure the hose using sticks, string, and tape so that it is firm and tight. There should be no gap between the hole and the base plate.

6 Cut a piece of paper that has the same oval shape as the mold's inside edge. Put the lion's head on the paper and trace the outline. Draw where the brackets for the lion are to be hung.

7 Mix concrete according to the instructions on the bag. Fill the mold with concrete and smooth the surface with a trowel. Tap to remove the air bubbles (see tips on page 143). Remove the sticks and place the paper template on the concrete. Stick down the suspension hooks and add pins for support so that the hooks will not fall. Let concrete cure for 3–4 days.

8 Tear away the form when the concrete has hardened. The lion's head's back plate is now done.

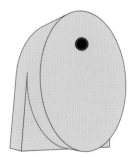

[Mold and reinforcement for the ground]

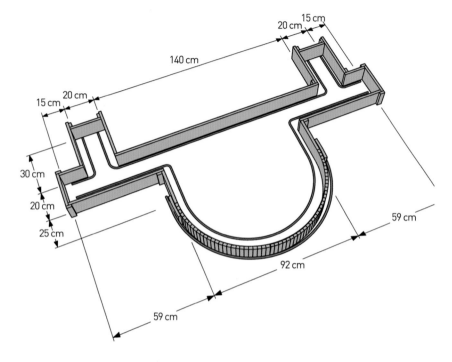

1 Take the MDF piece that is 12 x 145 cm (B).

2 Cut the wooden profiles in the lengths shown in the sketch. Cut the batten into 12 cm-long pieces.

3 Nail together wooden profiles, batten, and the traced MDF strip as shown.

4 Bend and nail a 3.2 m long rebar around the traced MDF strip for extra stability.

5 Cut and bend the reinforcing bars as shown in the sketch. There should be about 5 cm of free space to the mold wall.

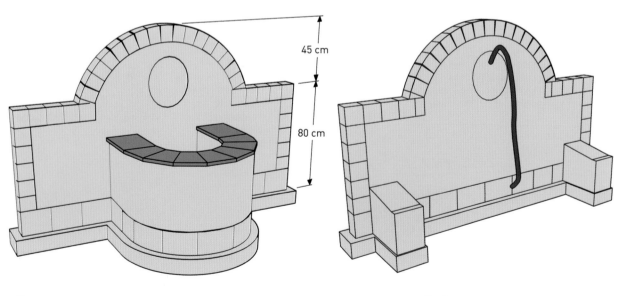

Front   **Back**

[Mold and reinforcement for the water reservoir]

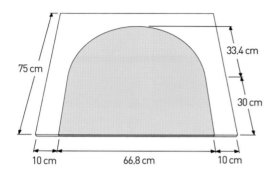

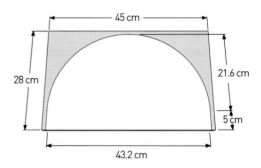

1 Bring out the two particle board pieces that are 75 x 87 cm (C1). Draw the water reservoir's outer contour on one of the discs as shown above (see also page 230). Cut out the pieces. The gray portion becomes waste. Work the second board in the same way. This will become the support discs to the rim of the reservoir.

2 Take out the two particle board pieces that are 45 x 28 cm (C2). Draw the water reservoir's inner contours on the pieces as shown above and cut them out. The gray portion becomes waste. Make the second disc in the same way. This will become the support discs for the inside edge of the reservoir.

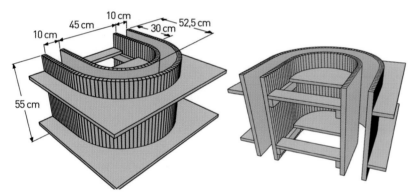

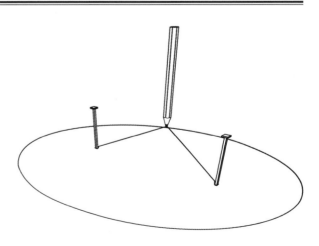

3 Pick up the pieces of the slotted MDF board that are 21 55 x 131 cm (C1) and 55 x 162 cm (C2). They will be used to mold the inner and outer edges. Build the mold according to the drawings of the concrete foundation. Cut out the pieces from what was left of the particle board and use it to nail the shape together.

4 Cut and bend eight rebars so that they fit the mold. Make sure that the rebars are not in contact with the inner and exterior walls.

Create an Ellipse

An ellipse is similar to an extended circle. The shape corresponds to an eccentric circle. The ellipse has two focal points. Since the sum of the distances from two foci to a point at the periphery is always the same, it is easy to create an ellipse with the help of two nails, a string, and a pen. The cord will be as long as the ellipse's major axis (long diameter), plus the distance between the foci. Be sure to include an allowance for attaching the cord to the nails. Put the nails in the foci. Tie the string into a loop and place the loop around the nails. Put the pencil inside the string loop and stretch the cord. Move the pen along the stretched string in both directions. Move the pen to the other side of the lace loop and draw the ellipse's second half in the same way.

[Lion's Head fountain]

1 Build the mold for the fountain base plate as described on the previous page. Place the completed form on the ground where the fountain is to be placed.

2 Mark the base plate form. A simple way is to mark the template mold with flour along its outer edges.

3 Dig out approximately 30 cm according to the line traced for the base.

4 Check that the mold fits into the pit. If not, adjust the pit. Pick up the mold. Line the pit with ground cloth. Fill half of it with gravel. Compress the gravel so that the surface is about 12 cm below ground level. Check it with a spirit level.

5 Put the mold on the compacted surface. Mix the concrete according to the directions on the bag. Fill up the mold halfway with concrete. Add in the bent rebars and top up with more concrete. Vibrate the concrete (see tip on page 143). Make the surface smooth by shaving off excess concrete with a board. Cover the concrete with plastic and let it cure for 3–4 days (see also page 43).

6 Mix the mortar according to the instructions on the bag. Start to build the fountain wall with a row of large pavement stones. The 25 cm-long pipe is to be cast in the middle row. The pipe allows water to travel from the container to the lion's head.

7 Continue building the fountain wall with Oppdal slate. Start and finish each layer with small cobblestones to even out the outer edge. Use the most beautiful stones at the front of the wall. Place the stones that are difficult to position in the sidewalls or in the back wall of the fountain (see illustration on previous page).

8 Place a sheet of plywood on the backside of the wall as a template for the fountain wall's top oval portion. Draw the desired shape of the top of your fountain.

9 Insert the lion's head's oval back piece in the middle of the top of the fountain wall. Use a number of small cobblestones to finish the top portion.

10 Place the mold for the water reservoir on the base plate directly next to the fountain wall.

11 Check the mold with a spirit level. I used waste wood to support the reservoir's rounded outer edge, but in the spec drawing of the shape, there are two discs that provide better support.

12 Seal the connection between the mold and the fountain wall with duct tape and plastic film so that the concrete does not leak out of the mold.

13 Fill the mold with concrete. Gradually add the eight bent rebars. Tap the concrete to remove air bubbles (see tip on page 143). Smooth the surface with a trowel and let the concrete cure for 3–4 days before the mold is demolished.

14 Decorate the water container's exterior with stones. Halve the large cobbles lengthwise (see tip on page 141). Mix the mortar. Lay a first layer with the halved pavement stones. Continue with small pieces of Oppdal slate.

15 Cut the sawn pieces of slate with a grinder to fit the reservoir's round facade. Lastly, bond the slate pieces into the shape of the top of the water reservoir.

16 Thread the 2 m garden hose from the fountain wall's backside partway through the cast tube stub in the fountain wall's bottom, and through the oval piece (see sketch on previous page).

17 Connect the garden hose with the lion's head by attaching the hose's upper end to the lion. Hang the lion's head on the oval cover.

18 Now it is time to add the adjustable fountain pump at the bottom of the water reservoir. Secure the garden hose to the pump connection. Seal the gap at the fountain wall with duct tape. Small holes are sealed with silicone. Fill the container with water and start the pump. Adjust the flow so that the stream of water arches in a nice shape and produces a beautiful tinkling sound.

ROMANTIC RUIN

A visit to Angkor Wat, Cambodia's city of ruins, made me fall head over heels in love with ruins. It was a completely magical experience to walk among the ruined temple of Ta Phrom. After centuries of oblivion and neglect, the jungle took over the building. Gigantic trees and roots have formed new walls beside old stone walls and natural ramparts surround religious relics. Just the thought of a small ruined wall surrounded by white flowers and partially hidden in the far corner of our garden makes me happy. To build your own romantic ruin, you'll need to plan and you'll need to have enough time and bricks. It may sound ridiculous, but the most important thing when building a ruin is preparing the foundation. After all, you want your newly built ruin to stand, colored with patina, for many, many years to come.

MATERIALS

FOR THE FOUNDATION
- 24 m² ground cloth
- 2.5 m³ crushed rock (⁰/₃₂)
- 0.5 m³ crushed rock (⁰/₁₂)

FOR THE MOLD
- 10 m boards (25 x 150 cm)
- 24 wood screws (4 x 40 mm)
- 6 brackets or 90 cm gusset

FOR THE RUIN WALL
- 600 kg coarse concrete
- 8.5 m rebar (10 mm)
- 5 m² protective plastic
- 300 kg mortar
- 380 second-hand bricks
- 3.6 m rebar (8 mm)
- 1 iron window (62 x 105 cm)
- 1 board (34 x 100 x 650 mm)
- 19 m battens (28 x 34 mm)
- Wood glue
- About 50 nails (35 x 1.7 mm)
- 2 pieces of Masonite (65 x 130 cm)
- 1.5 m flat bar steel to vault (30 x 5 mm)
- Black paint for iron and wood

FOR THE WHITE FLOWER BED
- 21 peat blocks (18 x 20 x 42 cm)
- 4 m² ground cloth
- 12.6 m rebar (8 mm)
- 1.5 m³ potting soil
- 40 liters packed gravel (⁶/₁₁)

Recycling
Used bricks will give the appearance of ruin and decay from the very start. Remove old mortar from the bricks with a mason's hammer before building.

STEP BY STEP

Select a suitable location and size for the ruin. Mine is 3.4 x I m. Measure and mark the ruin's contours with sticks and strings. If you wish to use different measurements, draw and adapt the amount of material according to the desired size of your ruin. Prepare the iron window and the two iron supports before working on the base.

1 Copy the arched window's upper shape on the 100 mm-wide board and cut out a curved frame section that is 28 mm wide. Cut the battening to fit it into a frame around the window's three straight edges. Cut a 10 mm-wide groove in the middle where the standing frame edges. Make a 10 mm joiner on the resting frame pieces' ends, so that they fit in the tracks.

2 Paint the frame pieces with black paint. Assemble the frame around the window. Glue together the joints. Paint the window frame a second time.

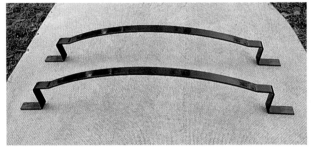

3 In the ruin wall, only one part of the window, the arched top, is covered with bricks. In order to lay the bricks steadily, two iron supports are required in the shape of the window arch. Let a smith or forging workshop bend two flat iron bars according to the window frame's arched shape. Bend the ends at a 90-degree angle so that the iron can be cast into the ruin wall. Paint the bent bars black.

4 Build the window into a box with the same width as the length of the bricks. Line the box with hardboard. In the picture, only half of the box is dressed to show how the window is placed in the middle of the box.

5 Dig a 60 cm-wide furrow into the ground down to the frost depth, at least 60 cm deep. It may be heavy work if there are a lot of stones or large roots. A mini-excavator will simplify the job. With some practice behind the levers, it is not difficult to dig with the scoop.

6 Our ground furrow is 90 cm deep. Line the bottom and walls with ground cloth. Fill the furrow with crushed rock. Flatten the gravel afterwards. Water and step on the stones. Finish with a layer of finely chopped gravel. The crushed stone should be level with the ground.

7 Tap the gravel with a hammer so that a flat and hard surface is created. You may need to add more crushed stone, and vibrate it once more to get the flat surface to the right level. Check with a spirit level so that the surface is more or less flat.

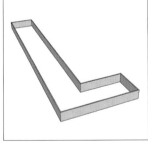

8 Build an L-shaped mold of wood for the ruin's base disc. The base disc should be 5–10 cm wider than the planned ruin wall. Add these margins for all sides—both the length of the disc and the width. Make the mold's walls 15 cm high.

[Casting the base]

1 My mold was 3.6 x 1.2 m on the long sides and 50 cm wide. Assemble the mold with angle brackets or corner plates in the corners.

2 Check the mold with a spirit level to ensure that the top edge is horizontal. Put clamps on the mold so that the walls do not fall out when the mold is filled.

3 Mix the concrete according to the instructions on the bag. Fill the mold halfway. Vibrate the concrete (see tips on page 143). Cut and bend 2 rebars (10 mm) in at a 90-degree the mold.

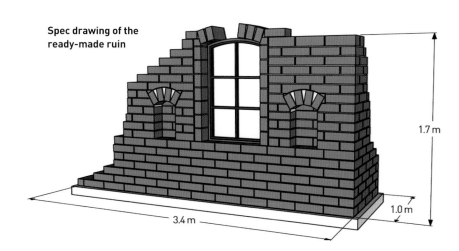

4 Fill up the rest of the form with concrete. Vibrate it by hand with a rebar as you go.

5 Remove any excess concrete with the edge of a plank. Cover the casting with plastic and let the concrete cure for 3–4 days. Water the concrete occasionally to slow the curing and the concrete will become stronger.

TOOLS

- Cord and marking pegs
- Yardstick or tape measure
- Mason's hammer
- Spade and/or mini excavators (available for rent)
- Wheelbarrow
- Scissors
- Soil compressor
- Spirit level
- Saw
- Clamps (50 cm)
- Chisel
- Knife
- Screwdriver
- Hammer
- Concrete mixer
- Bucket
- Trowel and caulking trowel
- Angle grinder, with wheels for cutting stone and metal
- Brush
- Shovel
- Saw
- Bolt cutter
- Small sledgehammer

Spec drawing of the ready-made ruin

1.7 m

1.0 m

3.4 m

Primula vulgaris mura

[Build the ruined wall]

1 Mix the mortar according to the directions on the bag. Start to build the ruin wall's corners. It should be two bricks wide, with a half brick displacement (read more on page 139). Bond the stones and continue building the entire first layer, brick by brick. Then bond them layer by layer.

2 When the wall is 50–60 cm high, reinforce it. Bend the rebar (8 mm) at a 90-degree angle and insert it between two brick rows. The iron is cast to stabilize the wall. Continue building the wall until you reach the height where the window is to be installed, approximately 65 cm up.

3 Place the window mold on the ruin wall. Fix the boards so they are secure. Place a brick on its edge with the long side facing the window. The bricks that stand against the window should always stand on their edge (see sketch on previous page).

4 Bond a window niche that has the same depth as the brick is wide (see illustration on previous page). The niche is the same height as the window's bottom edge. Putting tea lights in the niche at night will give it a lovely charm. Use bricks to support the building arch. Remove the support when the mortar has cured.

5 Remove the window mold's outer casing when you begin to reach the window's top edge. Place the two iron supports on the top arch and measure where the protruding pieces will end up in relation to the bricks.

6 Adjust these bricks to the iron's form. I had to cut out some notches in the top bricks so that the iron's top edge would be level with the arched top edge.

7 Bond together horizontal bricks on their edges as an arch over the window. The ruin will look more authentic if the arch is not completed.

8 The ruin is complete. All that remains is to give it a beautiful frame. My ruin stands in a rather dark corner. Therefore, the choice fell on white flowering plants.

[The white flower bed]

1 Begin by digging away the lawn—remove roots and loosen the existing soil with a garden fork. Top it up with potting soil of good quality.

2 The flower bed's edge is built of peat blocks. Put the blocks in the shade and cover them if they are not yet in use. This way they will retain moisture better.

3 Cut 40 cm strips of ground cloth. Put the strips where the peat blocks are to be placed. Place the peat blocks on top of the ground cloth, around the edge. The ground cloth should stick out 20 cm outside the blocks.

4 Adjust the shape of the peat blocks with a hand saw so that they lie close together.

5 The peat blocks need to be fixed to the ground. Cut 60 cm pieces of rebar with a bolt cutter and sharpen one end with the angle grinder.

6 Pound a rebar down into and through each peat block. Lean the rebars obliquely inwards towards the flowerbed. Beat them all the way into the peat blocks' top edge with a small hammer. The peat edge is complete.

7 An American yew and an azalea were already in my flowerbed. The maple was re-planted and tied up against two sturdy poles, with an elastic band for support until it is firmly rooted.

8 Add a few large stones to the peat edge for an interesting contrast.

9 Cover the entire flower bed with good potting soil.

10 Plant the plants and water them properly so that the roots make good contact with the soil. At twilight, magical white flowers will grow around the romantic ruin.

11 Peel off the grass. Add a 2 cm-thick macadam layer on the uncovered ground cloth. The gravel gives the flower bed a nice finish and reduces the risk of wild grass encroaching into the peat blocks.

MAGICAL WHITE FLOWERS AT DUSK

1. Elderberry

2. Goat's beard

3. Lily of the Valley

4. English Ivy

5. Snowy Barrenwort

6. Azalea 'Persil'

7. Woodruff

8. White Turk's Cap Lily

9. Christmas Rose

10. Primrose

11. Hosta 'Undulata'

12. Hosta 'June'

13. Western Bleeding Heart 'Alba'

14. Foxglove 'Snowy Mountain '

15. English Yew 'Repandens'

16. Hosta 'Halcyon'

17. Smooth Hydrangea 'Annabelle'

18. Astilbe 'Brautschleier'

19. Foam Flower

20. Solomon's Seal

21. Ostrich Fern

22. Drummond Norway Maple

23. Daffodil 'Mount Hood'

24. Grape Hyacinth 'White Magic'

25. Hyacinth 'Carnegie'

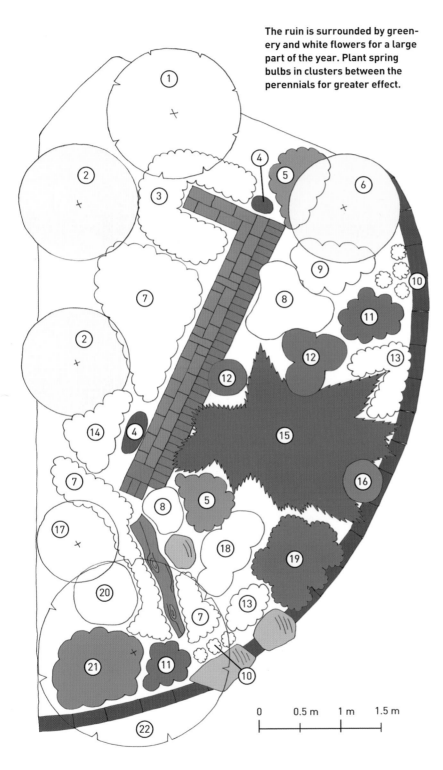

The ruin is surrounded by greenery and white flowers for a large part of the year. Plant spring bulbs in clusters between the perennials for greater effect.

0   0.5 m   1 m   1.5 m

PLANTS

1. Elderberry, *Sambucus nigra* (1 pc)
2. Goat's beard, *Aruncus dioicus* (2 pcs)
3. Lily of the Valley, *Convallaria majalis* (8 pcs)
4. English Ivy, *Hedera helix* (2 pcs)
5. Snowy Barrenwort, *Epimedium youngianum* 'Niveum' (13 pcs)
6. Azalea, *Rhododendron* 'Persil' (1 pc)
7. Woodruff, *Galium odoratum* (17 pcs)
8. White Turk's Cap Lily, *Lilium martagon* (8 pcs)
9. Christmas Rose, *Helleborus niger* (3 pcs)
10. Primrose, *Primula vulgaris* (7 pcs)
11. Hosta, *Hosta* 'Undulata' (10 pcs)
12. Hosta, *Hosta* 'June' (4 pcs)
13. Western Bleeding Heart, *Dicentra formosa* 'Alba' (9 pcs)
14. Foxglove, *Digitalis purpurea* 'Snow Mountain' (5 pcs)
15. English Yew, *Taxus baccata* 'Repandens' (1 pc)
16. Hosta, *Hosta* 'Halcyon' (1 pc)
17. Smooth Hydrangea, *Hydrangea arborescens* 'Annabelle' (1 pc)
18. Astilbe, *Astilbe arendsii* 'Brautschleier' (3 pcs)
19. Foam Flower, *Tiarella cordifolia* (6 pcs)
20. Solomon's Seal, *Polygonatum multiflorum* (3 pcs)
21. Ostrich Fern, *Matteuccia struthiopteris* (5 pcs)
22. Drummond Norway Maple, *Acer platanoides*, 'Drummondii' (1 pc)
23. Daffodil, *Narcissus pseudonarcissus* 'Mount Hood'
24. Grape Hyacinth, *Muscari aucheri* 'White Magic'
25. Hyacinth, *Hyacinthus orientalis* 'Carnegie'

CHAPTER 6

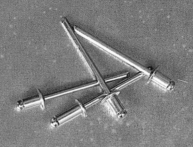

BENDING IRON, STEEL, AND WIRE

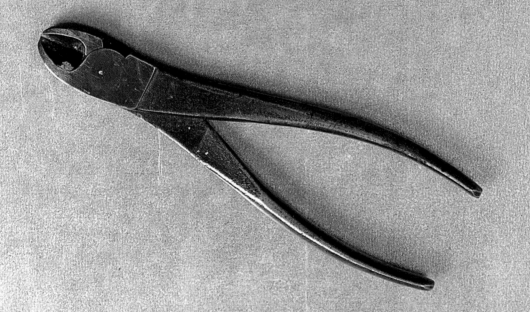

Strong as steel

While iron and steel are strong and sturdy materials, they are also soft and bendable, and make practical plant supports. Using rusty rebars in your garden will give it a rural, rustic feel. For a different effect, you can choose to paint the rebars black. In this chapter, I will also demonstrate how to bend shiny metal sheets into fancy pots and how to weave thin steel wires to make an attractive harvest basket.

Precision steel tubes are available in both round and square shapes.

Reinforcing steel has a fluted surface.

Galvanized steel wire in different dimensions.

Great-grandmother's bread pricker (a Swedish tool for making crispbread, known as a brödnagg) she bought from a vagabond many years ago.

Gold and silver metals have an alluring glimmer and are often used to create precious, beautiful items. Gold and copper in particular are so soft that you can work them with simple tools. People have discovered hammered copper jewelry that is over 10,000 years old. Today, since it is no longer common to use pure and precious metals in the garden, iron is an excellent substitute.

Cheap and Good

Iron is extracted from ores and is a relatively inexpensive material. However, the extraction process is tedious and it consumes a lot of resources.

Pig iron, or raw iron, is produced in smelting furnaces, which contain varying percentages of carbon. If the carbon content is reduced to below 2%, the iron becomes malleable.

Steel is an alloy that consists mainly of iron. Steel with small amounts of alloying elements is called non-alloy steel or carbon steel.

This simple unalloyed steel is used in rebars and rods, which are very useful in the garden.

Reinforcing steel is known as "rebar" in everyday speech. It is cheap, durable, and blends well in the garden. You can use rebars as plant supports or simple trellises.

In this chapter, we will also build with iron in sheet and wire forms.

Bending Metal

Functional and decorative objects that are made of metal are formed by hammering. It takes time and requires both skill and artistry.

I got the idea to bend metal to form simple shapes from a TV program featuring origami, the ancient art of folding paper into three-dimensional objects. I started experimenting with a square piece of paper and made simple creases in it, in order to find out how a metal sheet would look when worked in the same way.

Cutting and bending sheets of metal is the foundation of my metalwork. In order to bend and process plates with common tools, the sheet should not be too thick. A metal sheet thickness 0.5–1 mm is suitable.

Thin sheet metal may have very sharp edges. By folding the edge of the plate and hammering it out, you can blunt the edge and also strengthen the sheet. These types of edges are called wrapper edges.

Hobo Craft

One or two pairs of pliers and some wire is all you need to create functional and beautiful objects in wirework.

In the 1600s, it was common in southern Europe for vagabonds to repair damaged pottery with wire. Since then, technology has developed and advanced wirework is now used for both functional and decorative purposes.

In Scandinavia, the hobo walked through courtyards and offered to perform wirework in exchange for a meal and a place to sleep. It is thus not surprising that making objects from wire is also called hobo craft. However, the tradition of wire craft is not confined to Europe. In Africa, people make toys from recycled wire, and in South America it is common to bend wires made of more precious metals into beautiful jewelry.

Wire is available in varying thicknesses and metals. For hobo craft, steel wire works just fine. There is wire that is stiff and rigid, but wires that are annealed become softer. When annealing, a black oxide layer is created on the surface of the wire, which provides rust protection. The annealed wire may be used in indoor wirework whenever you might need a black thread.

It is best to use galvanized wire for outdoor wirework. Galvanized wire has a coat of zinc that prevents corrosion. Soft, annealed, or galvanized wires of different thicknesses are therefore very useful in wirework. Wire used for welding is rigid and not annealed, and is suitable for use as base wire in larger wirework projects, since it does not deform easily.

Purchasing Your Materials

Rebar is available in well-stocked DIY stores. Most often, they are sold in lengths of 6 m. It is best to get them cut to the right length in the store to facilitate the transport home.

Steel wire for hobo craft is available from specialist retailers in the home, leisure, or technology sections.

Steel sheets and bars are available at iron, steel, and metal shops.

The word "origami" is Japanese and means paper folding. With a single paper square, origami masters create the most amazing pieces. This art has a long tradition in Japan, and today there are countless variations of origami paper—in beautiful colors and patterns—available for purchase.

The crane, *orizuru*, is one of the most famous and popular origami figures. The crane is the symbol of happiness and long life—according to legend, anyone who folds a thousand cranes has their greatest wish fulfilled. To fold such a detailed crane in steel is unthinkable; however folding a simple, stylized steel bird is possible.

SAFETY

A risk when working with iron and steel is the actual cutting of the metal. Use great caution and work quietly and methodically.

• Wear heavy work gloves, and eye and ear protection when cutting with an angle grinder.

• Be careful that sparks from the angle grinder do not ignite dry materials. A leather apron protects clothes.

• Metal splinters and steel edges are often sharp. Use heavy work gloves to protect hands from cuts.

A rotating serving plate is an excellent tool when making a basket of wirework (see page 193). Place the work on the spinning plate so that you can sit in one place and braid the spiral binding on the sides of the rack while the plate is spun around.

TEEPEE FLOWER SUPPORT FOR CLEMATIS

Using rebar in the garden is both stylish and practical. Rebars are inexpensive, sturdy, and very durable. Unlike many other supports, rebars are rarely broken by plants or the weather. The natural rust color blends well with plant stalks and stems, so the rebar will be a discreet element in the flower bed. You can make a simple teepee plant support in a few minutes. The inspiration for the support comes from the teepee—a cone-shaped tent that the Native Americans of the Great Plains lived in during the 1800s. My teepee support consists of four rebars and wrapping wire.

MATERIALS

- 4 rebars, each 2 m (10 mm)
- 20 cm steel wire (1.5 mm)

TOOLS

- Bolt cutter
- Sledgehammer
- Needle-nose pliers
- Wire cutters

PLANTS

- Virgin's Bower, *Clematis viticella* 'Södertälje'

STEP BY STEP

It doesn't get simpler than this. Four rebars are held together at the top with wire. Clematis climbs by itself, but if it gets too big, it may need to be tied to the support with string.

1 In good potting soil, dig a pit for your clematis that has been watered. Place the rebars in a square around the plant; keep a distance of 30 cm between each rebar. Angle the rebars toward the center of the square and hammer them into the ground to a depth of at least 40 cm.

2 With your hand, hold the rebars together 10–15 cm from the top. Wrap wire 5–6 times around the rebars.

3 Twist the ends of the wire with needle–nose pliers so the wire is taut and the rebars sit together firmly.

4 Trim the ends of the wire with wire cutters. The simple teepee support is complete.

Fancy Blooms

Clematis belongs to genus *Ranunculus*, which consists of about 350 species, each of which has countless varieties. Some are shrubs while others are perennials. The size of clematis can vary from a couple of inches to over 10 m, and its flowers can grow to more than 20 cm in length. There are early flowering, summer flowering, and autumn flowering varieties with single, semi-double, and double flowers.

Many species climb by spinning their petioles around supports. Most climbing varieties require sun and heat.

If you plant the water-drenched clematis 10 cm deeper than it was planted in the pot, it will develop new shoots and roots along the stem. If you cut its length down to 20 cm right at the time of planting, it will establish roots much easier. The clematis gets thirsty and hungry easily, so provide it with water and nutrition regularly. Plant it beside low-growing plants to shadow the clematis at ground level, so that evaporation is reduced.

Since some varieties bloom off the previous year's shoots and some flower on new shoots, different types of pruning are required. Clematis can be divided into three different pruning groups. Group 1 requires light pruning after bloom where weak and dead branches are removed. In Group 2, dead and damaged branches are removed in early spring, but you should also cut healthy shoots down to more robust shoots. For Group 3, cut all branches in early spring to be 15–30 cm above the ground.

'Rouge Cardinal'

'Pixie'

'Pink Flamingo'

'Multi Blue'

Alpine Clematis

SPIDER WEB

Some animals use sophisticated methods to obtain their food. The spider, for example, spins a fine web to capture its prey. During the early morning, the silk of the spider's web is covered with dew. The morning sun glistens in the water droplets, and the spider web shines like a strand of jewels among blades of grass. The threads of the spider web are thin and fragile, but the entire web is durable and elastic. Mimic the spider and create your own web of steel wire. In only a few hours, you can create a spider web in an apple tree that will glisten beautifully in the sun. Using the same technique, you can also bind a small wire box for suet balls to feed the birds, as is described in the next section.

MATERIALS

- 7.2 m galvanized steel wire (1.5 mm)
- 25 m galvanized steel wire (0.7 mm)

TOOLS

- Wire cutters
- Needle-nose pliers

STEP BY STEP

Locate a good space between the branches of an apple tree. In my tree, there was about 50 cm between the upper and lower branches, and my spider web was 32 cm in diameter.

1 Cut the thick steel wire into six pieces. Each piece should be 1.2 m long. These will be the base wires of the web. Be gentle with the tree when tightening the wires. Make a loose loop around the branch so as not to damage it.

2 Continue tightening the base, wire by wire. Ensure that all base wires intersect in the web's center.

3 Use thin steel wires for the web. Cut a 10 cm-long piece. In the middle of the web, wrap it twice around one of base wires. Then, weave it around the next base wire and so on until all are connected.

4 Cut pieces of the thin steel wire that are approximately 2 m long. Start weaving the rest of the spider web 2 cm from the center of the web. Begin and end each circle with an extra lap around the base wire. Lastly, remove any wire ends that are sticking out. The homemade spider web is ready.

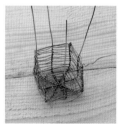

Suet Ball Birdfeeder

Remove the boring plastic net from the suet ball and make a wire box with the same material as the spider web. You'll need 2.8 m of base wire (1.5 mm wide) and 5 m of weaving wire (0.7 mm wide). Cut seven base wires of 30 cm each. Bend three of them into three squares, 6 x 6 cm in size. Form the remaining four base wires in a cross and weave a base 6 x 6 cm square. Bend the base wires in a 90-degree angle and insert one of the square supports. Continue by weaving the walls of the holder. Finish by wrapping a square firmly to the top. The third square is the body to a separate lid that is the same size as the bottom, but with four base wires that are 10 cm. Pop in a suet ball and fasten the lid and the cube with wrapping wire. Hang it in a tree and watch the birds eat.

FLOWER VASE HOLDER

A small floral bouquet that hovers just below the crown of a tree catches the eye better than a vase placed on the table. The iron holder that supports the vase has been bent around an oak rod. A large hook at the top lets you hook the vase onto the branches of a tree. Also, you'll see that the shape of the holder matches the conical concrete candleholders on page 61. Floating flowers and candles will create a warm, fairy-like atmosphere during the evening.

MATERIALS

- 1 round iron rod, 65 cm (6 mm)

TOOLS

- Bolt cutter
- 15 cm round oak rod (50 mm)
- Drill driver
- Drill bit (6 mm)
- Bending machine
- Pipe wrench
- Metal file

PLANTS

- Climbing rose, *Rosa* 'Flammentanz'

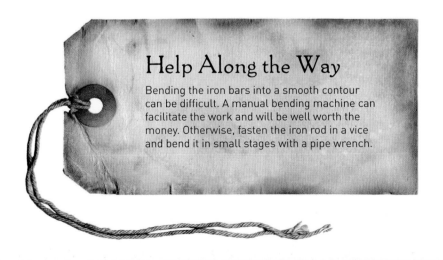

Help Along the Way

Bending the iron bars into a smooth contour can be difficult. A manual bending machine can facilitate the work and will be well worth the money. Otherwise, fasten the iron rod in a vice and bend it in small stages with a pipe wrench.

STEP BY STEP

Bend the iron rod around a coarse, solid oak rod to form the loop that will hold the vase. Before you begin, drill a hole in the oak rod; the hole should be in the middle of the oak rod's long side and should be about 6 mm wide and about 2.5 cm deep.

1 Cut a 65 cm-long piece of iron rod (if it's not precut).

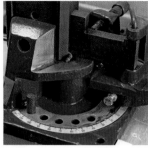

2 Use a bending machine to bend 2 cm of one end of the bar at a 90-degree angle.

3 Insert the bent end into the hole in the oak rod.

4 Place the round oak rod on a flat surface and grip it with a pipe wrench.

5 Use the pipe wrench to twist the oak rod so the iron rod wraps once around it.

6 Snip the bent piece of iron rod that is inserted in the oak; remove the oak rod.

7 You now have the ring that will hold the vase.

8 Use the bending machine to bend the iron shaft at a 90-degree angle.

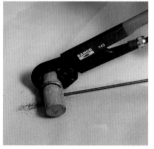

9 Bend the opposite end of the iron rod to make a loop for hanging. File down any sharp edges.

10 The holder is ready and can be hung in the tree.

Classic Pink Beauties

'Maiden's Blush' has cute round buds, and the flower is light pink with a yellow eye. Its foliage is blue-green, which is the characteristic of many Alba roses.

'Rosa Mundi' is a streaked gallicaros first cultivated in the 1500s.

'Nuits de Young' is a moss rose with deep reddish-purple flowers that appear especially striking against white cast iron furniture.

'William Lobb' is a moss rose and its conspicuous buds are well worth studying up close.

'Pink Grootendorst' is, despite its friendly look, a tough rose with many thorns. It is a carnation rose belonging to the *Rosa rugosa* species of rose.

'Charles de Milles' is a dense and eager-to-bloom gallica rose with large, full, and slightly flat pink flowers.

A Budding Rose

Is the modern shrub rose 'Golden Wings' not pretty in all of its stages? First it shows its perfect bright yellow buds. Shortly after, it opens up its delicate pale yellow petals. Before the leaves fall to the ground, we enjoy its lovely pale yellow flower in full bloom.

HANGING PLANTER WITH "EARS"

Summer flowers that hang in planters at the entrance of your house always look welcoming. And because they hang at eye level, the pot is very visible. We used to have simple white planters made of plastic, but after a season they looked sullied and dreary. If you want unique planters, you can make them yourself out of steel. The sun glistens beautifully when it hits the reflective metal, and the planter's curved shape gives it a unique appearance. I've also realized that deer love pansies. They eat not only the flowers, but they'll also drag up the plants and leave them to wither on the ground. It's so sad to see! Deny the deer their snack and hang your pansies in a metal planter so that you get to enjoy their floral splendor for longer.

MATERIALS

- 1 hot-dip galvanized steel sheet 0.6 mm (70 x 70 cm)
- 25 cm galvanized steel wire (2 mm)
- 10 liter potting soil
- Chain for hanging

TOOLS

- Ruler
- Yardstick or spirit level
- Shears
- Awl
- Hammer
- Drill driver
- Drill bit (4 mm)
- Clamps
- Wooden wedge and protection board

PLANTS

- Pansy, *Violax wittrockiana* (4 pcs)

STEP BY STEP

The metal sheet can be purchased from stores that sell iron, steel, and metal. You can often buy whole plates at 1 x 2 m. It may be possible to obtain smaller pieces from metal recycling companies.

1 Place the steel sheet on a flat surface. Measure and draw a square that is 70 x 70 cm, if you didn't get the sheet precut.

2 Cut the metal sheet with manual or pneumatic shears.

3 Measure and mark the center with a yardstick, or as seen here with a spirit level.

4 With an awl and hammer, form a notch at the center point mark. Drill a hole through the plate.

5 Place the sheet on a workbench; 5 mm should stick out from the edge of the bench. Use a board to protect the sheet and fasten the boards and metal sheet to the workbench with clamps.

6 Take a small wooden board and put it against the edge of the sheet. Hammer down on the steel sheet so the edge bends. Keep hammering on the edge until the edge is bent at a 90-degree angle.

7 Remove the board and continue tapping the edge so it folds down flat on the backside of the sheet. Repeat the process on the other three edges.

8 Place the sheet diagonally on the workbench; it should lie over the edge of the workbench. Cover with a board for protection, and fasten both the board and the sheet to the workbench with clamps.

9 Use another board to bend down the section of the sheet that projects over the side.

10 Remove the wooden board from the metal and continue bending the steel sheet until it is fully folded.

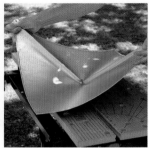

11 Lastly, cover the sheet again with a board and fix both the board and the sheet to the workbench with clamps; this will help bend the sheet more completely.

12 Remove the wooden board from the workbench. Insert a wooden wedge between the folded halves of the sheet and pry the plate apart once more.

13 Gently bend the plate halves by hand until the plate is almost entirely flat.

14 Flip the sheet over. Grip the metal corners that were originally bent and press the corners of the sheet toward each other.

15 Shape the two "ears" of the planter; do this by hand and with smooth movements to prevent any creases from forming.

16 Form the middle divider by squeezing the metal by hand.

17 Drill a hole at the top edge of each ear. Make sure it goes through both of the pieces of metal. Thread a piece of wire through the holes and bend it into a loop for hanging. Drill a drainage hole the bottom of each ear. Now the planter is ready for the flowers.

18 Fill the trellis with potting soil and mix it well with a small amount of long-acting fertilizer. Plant the plants and water thoroughly.

Practice Planter

It's very difficult to revive a sheet that was bent improperly. A quick practice attempt before you start bending your planter is a good idea, so first try to form a similar shape in paper. Paper is more forgiving, and if a fold goes wrong, you can simply redo it.

To do this:
Cut an 20 x 20 cm sheet of paper. Mark the center on the sheet. Fold the paper diagonally. Unfold the paper again and turn it upside down. Grab the corners where the fold was made and squish the corners so the paper bends over the center and the corners meet. The planter's "ears" are now created.

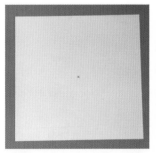
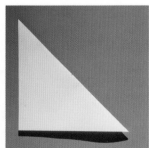

SHEET METAL POT

Down at the local boating club, small boats are lined up in a row beside the bridge. Ducks swim calmly among the swaying reeds. This marine environment is adorned with many sleek, manicured materials—a shiny white plastic hull; glossy, varnished teak decks; bollards of stainless steel; and smoke-colored glass, just to name a few. At the end of the beautifully-weathered dock, a steel pot would look right at home. This pot has three sections that have been assembled like a flower with six petals. At the end of my instructions, there's a section on how a planter can be hung on a wall.

MATERIALS

- 3 hot-dip galvanized metal sheets 0.6 mm (70 x 70 cm)
- 6 rivets
- 30 cm galvanized steel wire (1.5 mm)
- 30 liters potting soil

TOOLS

- Ruler
- Yardstick or spirit level
- Shears
- Drill driver
- Drill bit (4 mm)
- Clamps
- Rubber mallet
- Hand riveter
- Cutting pliers

PLANTS

- Heather, *Calluna vulgaris* 'Knospenbluher' (12 pcs)

Elegant with Rivets

Attaching rivets to sheet metal is simple and the result is quite elegant. You don't need sophisticated tools; a drill and a hand riveter are sufficient.

STEP BY STEP

When buying sheet metal, you'll likely find four sheets that are each 70 x 70 cm. Use three of them to construct this pot and use the fourth to make a wall planter. Check out my wall pot in the picture on the next page. Simply join the front part of the sheet with the back part and make a loop out of steel wire to hang the planter.

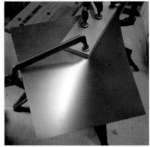

1 Measure and cut three sheets to 70 x 70 cm, or buy them precut. Work with one sheet at a time.

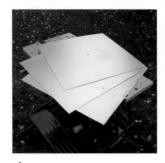

2 Drill a hole in the middle of the sheet. Place the hole over the corner of the workbench. The sheet should lie diagonally. Place a wooden board on top of the sheet and clamp both the board and the sheet to the table. Bend the plate at a 90-degree angle along the edge of the bench; do this by hammering it down with a rubber mallet.

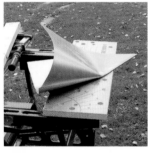

3 Unclamp the sheet from the workbench. Continue pounding and bending until a sharp fold is formed.

4 Gently bend the sheet halves back so that the sheet opens up around the crease.

5 Align the crease along the edge of the work-bench with the center hole on the bench's corner. Hold the sheet against the bench. Gently push down the side pro-truding from the workbench; do this by hand so the sheet folds down.

6 Return the sheet to the workbench. Hold the bent edge of the sheet with a firm grip; press it down against the flat side of the sheet. The first section, with its two petals, is now complete.

7 Prepare the other two sheets in the same man-ner; you should now have three equal sections. These three sections should now be placed back to back and attached together with rivets.

8 To do this, clamp together two adjacent metal walls. Drill a hole through the sheets, about 1 cm from the edge and 10 cm from the center of the pot.

9 Insert a rivet in the hole and rivet the sheets together. Rivet together the two remaining sections in the same way. Add more rivets along the edge, 10 cm below the first rivet.

10 Now, the section's inner walls should be attached at the center of the pot "flower." Drill a hole in each partition, approximately 2 cm from the tip and 1 cm in from the outer edge.

11 Also drill a hole at the tops of the riveted metal sheets. Position the holes so they match the height of the holes on the inner walls.

12 Thread wire through the holes in the sheets and pull to tighten the sheets together. Twist the wire and trim the ends.

13 Drill a drainage hole at the bottom of each section of the pot.

14 Now the metal pot is ready for planting. Fill the sections with potting soil, and plant and water the flowers.

Wall Planter

A bare, boring outdoor wall can be easily livened up. Using leftover sheet metal, make an extra planter with two petals. It will become a beautiful ornament to hang on a wall.

PLANTS
- Hairy Alumroot, *Heuchera villosa* 'Palace Purple' (2 pcs)
- Creeping Jenny, *Lysimachia nummularia* 'Goldilocks' (2 pcs)

The Heather Queen

Calluna vulgaris is the scientific name of heather. Vulgaris is Latin and it means ordinary. The word calluna probably descended from the Greek word kalluno which means to sweep. In the past, heather was used in brooms.

Heather is a small vine–like shrub that is commonly found in nutrition-poor, dry soils. Its stems are often twisted and bent. Its leaves look like small needles, and its flowers are usually pink and gathered in bunches. Processed varieties exist in other colors.

The roots of heather are tough and strong and have been used in basket weaving. Heather can even be used to dye yarn to brown, yellow, and red hues. Heather produces a lot of nectar and is an important plant for beekeepers.

Nectar gathered from heather produces a dark yellow honey.

Heather, *Calluna vulgaris* 'Silver Knight'

Stuart's Heather, *Erica x stuartii* 'Irish Lemon'

Erica gracilis

HARVEST BASKET

One of the highlights of the spring, summer, and autumn is to harvest the garden's treasures. It is a delight to wander around the garden, harvesting vegetables and berries for dishes and picking flowers to decorate the table. Fresh fruits and vegetables can be picked and put into a hand-crafted harvest basket. Some pliers and wire are all that's needed to create this beautiful, spacious harvest basket using wirework.

MATERIALS

FOR THE TEMPLATE
- 1 piece of plywood (65 x 50 cm)
- 32 cm wooden staff (10 mm)
- 1 planed timber batten (16 x 45 x 300 mm)
- 3 wooden flower sticks of 50 cm (5 mm)

FOR THE BASKET
- 9 m galvanized steel wire (2 mm)
- 23 m galvanized steel wire (0.7 mm)
- 54 m galvanized steel wire (1.5 mm)

TOOLS
- Saw
- Ruler or tape measure
- Drill driver
- Drill bits (2 mm, 5 mm, and 10 mm)
- Hammer
- Protractor
- Utility knife
- Wire cutters
- Needle-nose pliers
- Round-nose pliers
- 20 cm round bar (50 mm)

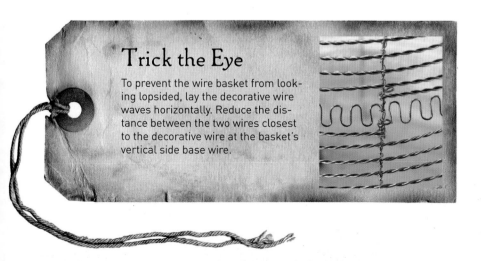

Trick the Eye

To prevent the wire basket from looking lopsided, lay the decorative wire waves horizontally. Reduce the distance between the two wires closest to the decorative wire at the basket's vertical side base wire.

STEP BY STEP

For your wirework to be successful, it's important to make good templates. If the templates are symmetrical, the product will also be symmetrical. Make the templates for the basket and the decorative waves first, so they'll be ready to use when the wiring process begins.

The template for the base's stamens and the template for the basket's top edge can be made on the same plywood board since they are not used simultaneously.

[Template for the frame's base wires]

The base of the basket is made of stamens. The stamen wires need to be bent around a number of pins before all the stamens will have the same shape.

1 Cut out 8 pieces of round rod that are 4 cm long. The rods will become the template's pins.

2 Transfer the measurements from the drawing to the plywood and mark where the pins will be located. Leave 5 mm between the three pins on the bottom so that the base wire can be wired between the pins.

3 Drill holes for the pins with a 10 mm drill and knock the pins into the holes.

[The template for the basket's top edge]

Fix the base wires at the basket's top edge to the plywood template to make it easier to make the basket.

1 Draw a circle 34 cm in diameter on the plywood board (see page 230).

2 Divide the circle into ten equal wedges. Preferably, use a protractor to measure out a 36-degree angle for the point of the wedge.

3 Drill holes in the disc at the intersections of the circle with a 2 mm drill so that it has 10 holes on the circumference of the circle.

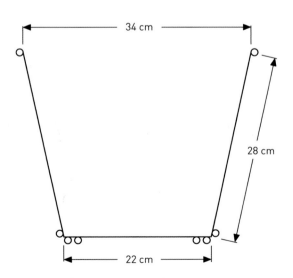

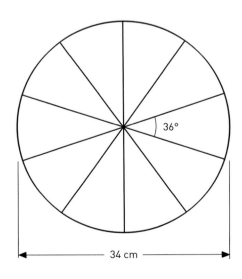

[Outline of the wave pattern]

To bend a wire so that it forms a wave, use a template with two parallel rows of staggered pins.

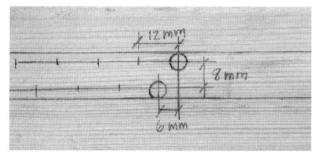

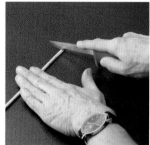

1 Draw two parallel lines with a distance of 8 mm between them. Then, mark pin placements on the two lines. The distance between the pins on the rows is 12 mm, and the pin placement on the two lines is offset by 6 mm in relation to each other. Drill a hole with a 5 mm drill bit at each mark.

2 Divide the flower pins into 2.5 cm-long pieces using a knife. Press the knife against the pin and roll it back and forth with the other hand. Break the pin at the cutting groove. These bits are the template's pins. You will need about 50 pins for a long template. Put the pins in the holes.

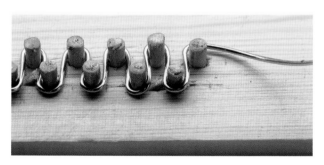

3 The template can be any length but not less than 10 pins in a row. The wave pattern is created by the thread, which is 1.5 mm in diameter. Bend this wire back and forth around the pins. When the wire is bent around all the pins, loosen it from the template. By shaping the last thread around the template's first pin, it is easy to continue with the wave pattern. Repeat this until the entire thread is done. The wave pattern can then be pulled or pressed together to shape the bends as you wish.

[Twist two wires]

1 Fasten two wires to the workbench or in a vice. Attach the other ends in a drill chuck.

2 Run the drill at low speed so it twists the wires elegantly. Note that the twisted thread will be about 10% shorter than the original wire length.

[Build the basket]

1 Cut 5 pieces of the 2 mm thick wire to be 1 m long. Bend one base thread at a time into the template. Bend a loop around the top pin. Then put the wire inside the second pin, outside the third and inside the fourth. Continue to follow the template and finish with a loop.

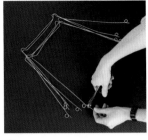

2 Carefully remove the curved wire from the template. Bend the remaining four wires in the same way. Trim off excess thread so that 1 cm is left outside the loops.

3 Take out the template for the basket's top edge and put the first base stamens in two opposite holes.

4 Insert the remaining base stamens into every other hole. Mark the center of the stamens with a marker pen to simplify the rest of the binding work.

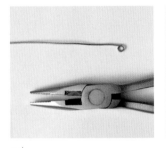

5 In order to link the stamens in the basket bottom, use 0.7 mm wire. This is what I call the wrapping wire. Cut a wire to a length of 1 m. Form a loop at the end of the wire with needle-nose pliers.

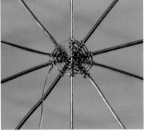

6 Temporarily release one of the stamens and thread the loop around it. Move the loop to the center of the basket. Wrap the wire around each stamen once so that an approximately 2 cm-wide spider web is formed. Let the end hang loose.

7 Cut 10 wrapping wires to a length of 1.5 m. Form loops at the end of the threads. Thread the loops onto each stamen the same way as before. Move them up towards the spider web pattern. Now there is a wrapping wire attached to each stamen around the spider web.

8 Wrap another round of web wire (see step 6) outside the loops so that they are attached to the web. When all loops are secured, spin the web wire two times around the end of the stamen and trim it off.

9 Cut a 4 m-long wire for the bottom's base. Use the wire that is 2 mm thick. Pre-bend the wire by spinning it around a coarse round wooden rod. Remove the wire from the rod.

10 Form a loop at one of the ends. Thread it onto one of the stamens. Place the loop towards the spider web and attach it with the stamen's wrapping wire. Continue to attach the base wire to each stamen with their individual wrapping wires. Make an extra lap with the wrapping wire around the stamens between each round.

11 Continue to attach the base wire to the stamens with the wrapping wire until the base wire covers the entire bottom of the basket. Cut the base wire close to the basket's bottom.

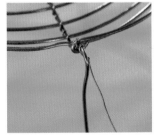

12 Finish by curling the cut wire around the post with needle-nose pliers. Secure the base wire with the wrapping wire.

13 The basket side's base spiral begins with rows of twisted wire. Twist together two 1.5 mm thick and 4 m long steel wires with a drill (see previous spread). Bend the twisted end of the wire into a loop.

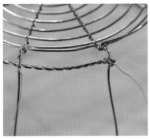

14 Thread the loop onto the stamen where the base twine ended. Attach the twined wire onto the stamen with the stamen's wrapping wire.

15 Shape the twisted wire into a helix around the basket. Attach the wire to each stamen with its respective wrapping wire. The twisted wire should reach five rounds around the basket. Cut the thread and finish in the same way as previously.

16 The next round on the basket will be a decorative wave using steel wire that is 1.5 mm thick. Bend the wire in a wave template until you have a wavy thread that is about 80 cm long. Cut the wire and form a loop at one end. Angle the loop at a 90-degree angle to the wave template.

17 Thread the loop onto the stamen where the twisted wire stopped and secure it with wrapping wire (see tip on page 193). Attach the wavy wire to each stamen with wrapping wires. End the lap in the same way.

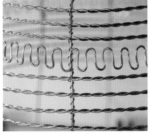

18 Make a new twisted wire from two pieces of 11 m steel wires. Form a loop. Thread the loop on the stamen where the wavy thread ended. Attach the twisted wire to each stamen with the wrapping wire in the same way.

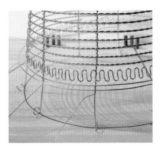

19 The twisted wire is enough for eleven laps around the basket. Weave another lap of wavy decorative wire and three laps of the single 1.5 mm-thick wire.

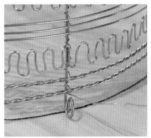

20 Weave another lap with the wavy wire. Finish the basket with some rounds of the twisted wire. I fitted in 3 laps, but adapt to the amount of space left. Attach them to the stamens in the same way.

21 Remove the basket from the template. Turn the basket so the bottom faces downward. Finish the basket with the last lap of twisted wire. Attach the wire to the stamens' loops with the wrapping wires.

22 Cut 6 pieces of 1.5 mm-thick wire into lengths of 60 cm each. Thread three of the threads through two adjacent loops and shape the wire into a handle. Place the ends at the top of the handle. Cut a 3.5 m-long wrapping wire and attach it further up on the handle.

23 Build up the handle by spinning the wrapping wire tightly around the thicker wires. Finish by cutting the wrapping wire and poke it inside the end of the handle. Proceed in the same way to make a handle on the opposite side.

24 Trim off the part of the stamen wires that are sticking out from the end loops. Secure the wrapping wire by wrapping them 3–4 extra laps around the stamens. Cut the wrapping wire. The basket is ready to be filled with freshly harvested vegetables.

CHAPTER Nº 7

WELDING IRON

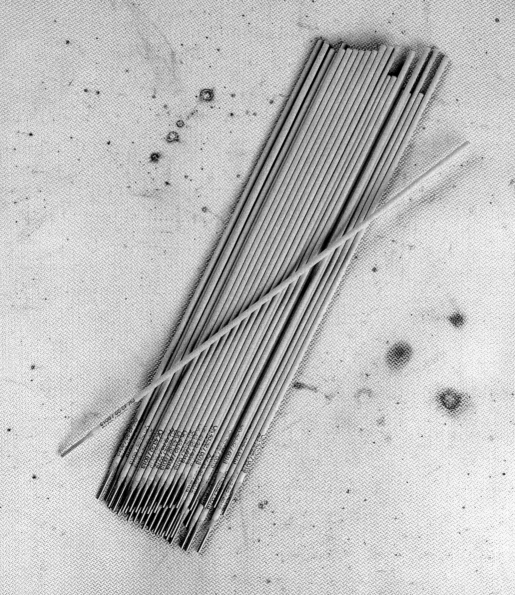

Strong & light

Welding is not usually a technology you would associate with the garden. However, welding will create many more possibilities for your garden projects. Where you had previously weaved wires together to make plant supports, with welding you can now make stable constructions in all shapes and sizes. I learned how to weld over a couple of months at an evening course.

The Golden Gate Bridge in California, a famous suspension bridge, was opened 1937. At that time it was the world's longest bridge. Its unique structure and characteristic red-orange color make it to stand out. Steel was manufactured on the East Coast and transported by train and boat to San Francisco, where it was then assembled. 2 m-thick and 2.3-kilometer-long cables support the bridge. The towers measure 227 m above sea level.

There are many ways to put together metal materials. One of these ways is welding. Metal pieces are heated up and fused together. The energy required to melt the materials is generated in different ways, using to different welding techniques. Advanced techniques make it possible to weld underwater and in space, and simpler techniques can be used for industrial welding, as well as welding in the garden. In arc welding, the materials should be free from dirt and oxides and the welding electrode should have a low moisture content to make a satisfactory weld.

This is the equipment you need to weld in the garden—a welder with an electrode and grounding conductor, a welding helmet, gloves, and a leather apron.

My Introduction to Welding

Welding is my most recently acquired skill. An advertisement for an evening course in my municipality sparked my interest. Although I had never had the equipment or basic skills to weld, I was curious to learn. For a few hours every week for the next few months, I gained a taste of welding. Now, I have acquired a small welder, and I weld plant supports and simple structures for the garden.

Arc Welding

I have a simple arc welder. The real name of the technology is metal arc welding, MMA (Manual Metal Arc). It's a simple but relatively slow welding method. The equipment consists of a power source, a welding cable with an electrode holder, and a return conductor. The electrode consists of core wires and a sheath. When welding, an arc of light appears between the electrode and the work piece by an electrical short. The arc makes the metal pieces melt. Among other things, the job of the electrode's cover is to produce protective dross.

In order to form an arc between the electrode and the goods, the grounding conductor has to be connected to what is to be welded.

A magnetic holder keeps the parts in place in a 90-degree angle and is an excellent support when welding.

Other Arc Welding Methods

Because it takes time to change the electrode and tap the dross, new welding methods have been developed where the wire is fed by a machine and a gas atmosphere protects the arc. The difference between MIG welding (Metal Inert Gas) and MAG welding (Metal Active Gas) is the gas or the gas mixture that is used. The equipment for MIG/MAG is more extensive and is used mainly by welding professionals in the industry.

Another high quality welding method used in the welding industry is TIG welding (Tungsten Inert Gas).

Risks and Quality Requirements

When welding, a flame with a very high temperature that can ignite most materials produced. Glowing spatter is dangerous, as are the "black" welding sparks, which may have a temperature of up to 500°C.

The noxious fumes contain a mixture of gases and metallic particles that evaporate from the hot arc and the melted metal.

Another risk with welding is the intense UV and IR radiation that is generated. Radiation is extremely harmful to your eyes and skin.

If you are you interested in welding you should definitely begin by attending a welding course. A simpler way is to enlist the help of a steel and welding company. You can decide what kind of iron and steel work you want and employ a company to do the welding itself.

The world's most famous steel structure is probably the Eiffel Tower, which was built for the World Exhibition in Paris in 1889. The 300 m-high tower was the world's tallest building for more than 40 years and is one of truss technology's masterpieces. Two and a half million rivets join various parts. Riveting was the dominant bonding method when the tower was built. In the early 1900s, welding was developed and the foundation of modern steel construction was created.

SAFETY

Welding is extremely flammable and must be handled accordingly. Ensure that sparks do not ignite other materials.

• A welding shield or welding helmet is mandatory. The intense ultraviolet radiation is harmful to the eyes.

• Wear heavy work gloves and a leather welding apron to protect your skin from radiation and sparks.

• Weld in an area with adequate ventilation so that you will not breathe in the unhealthy welding fumes.

• Work gloves, safety glasses, and hearing protection are required when cutting with an angle grinder.

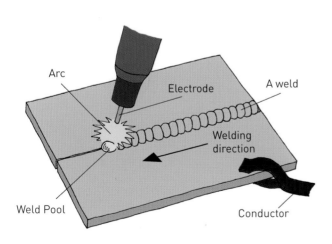

Spec drawing of a weld.

MOORESQUE VAULT

Walking through a fragrant rose arc or a door standing ajar is enticing. It frames the garden and gives it a lift. A softly rounded Moorish arch, which can be seen in the Great Mosque of Córdoba or in the magnificent Alhambra Palace outside Granada in Spain, creates a beautiful shape. An easy way to bring Moorish architecture into your garden is to bend rebars. Our slender Mooresque vault frames the Greek urn which sits on top of a stone (see p 143). An alternative to welding the iron rods is to wrap them together with lashing wire.

MATERIALS

- 1 sheet of plywood (10 x 750 x 1350 mm)
- 6 rebar 6 m (10 mm)
- Masking tape
- 1.5 m rebar (8 mm)
- 5 m strip of wood (30 mm wide)
- 12 small nails
- 1 piece of masonite (1 x 1 m)
- 12 m lashing wire

TOOLS

- Ruler
- Awl
- String (1 m)
- Scissors
- Jigsaw
- Tape measure
- 5 fast wings or clamps
- 1 long screw clamp (90 cm)
- 2 pipes 2 m (inner diameter 12.7 mm)
- Angle grinder or bolt cutters
- Bending machine or vise and pipe wrench
- Hammer
- 2.5 m elastic rope
- Spirit level
- Straightener
- Wire cutters
- Self-locking welding clamp
- Welding equipment; e.g. stud weld
- Wire brush
- Chipping hammer

STEP BY STEP

The vault is 90 cm-wide. Aligning several arches in a row will create an airy pathway. Arches can be dressed with annual climbers.

1 Draw two circles on the plywood board with diameters of 60 cm and 72 cm (see page 230). The cord loops need to be 30 cm and 36 cm long. Cut out the templates. They are needed to bend the arcs.

2 Make a datum point on the large template's periphery. Measure 1 m in each direction along the template's edge and make a new mark. The iron should be bent in this direction. In the same way, mark 70.7 cm from the datum mark on the small template.

3 Mark the center of the rebars with tape. Also mark how far the irons should be bent. Put a piece of tape 1 m in each direction on two irons and 70.7 cm on four irons.

4 Place the small circular template and one of the accompanying rebars on a workbench. Secure the midpoint of the rebar against the datum point on the template's periphery with clamps.

5 Secure the circular template to the workbench with clamps so that it sits firmly.

6 Put the iron pipes on the rebar's ends to meet the outer tape marks. Hold the iron pipes and begin to bend the iron around the template.

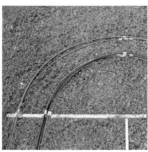

7 Bend the iron smoothly around the template's edge so that the markings on the iron reach the marks on the template.

8 Let go of the iron pipes. The rebar will then open up so that a semicircle with a diameter of 90 cm forms.

9 Loosen the clamps and remove the pre-bent iron. Bend the other three rebars in the same way and with the same template.

10 Bend the remaining two rebars after the great circle's template. Place the six bent bars on the lawn. There should be 17.5 cm between the small and the large arches.

11 Cut the small arcs to the same length as the big iron arches' lower edges. Put a tape mark 20 cm from the bottom on each rebar.

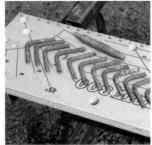

12 Cut twelve 12 cm-long pieces of rebar that are 8 mm in diameter. Bend the pieces at a 90-degree angle in a bending machine, or with a pipe wrench when they are secured in a vise.

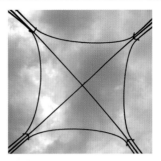

13 Assemble the iron arcs into a vault. Put the small arcs in an exterior square, and the large arcs should sit like an internal cross. Push the rebars gently into the ground. They should sit 3 cm away from each other. See also the sketch below.

14 Nail together simple 30 mm-wide spacers to a cross. Put the spacing pieces between the irons, 5 cm above the ground marks. Keep the irons together with elastic rope.

15 Fasten a framework of 30 mm-wide strips between the irons so that they are positioned at the right distance from each other. Check regularly that the irons are straight with a spirit level.

16 Cut out a 5 x 5 cm square from each corner on the masonite sheet. Place the masonite on the bars. Nudge the irons' placement so that they are firmly against the recesses. The masonite disc holds the irons parallel and at the right distance.

17 Tie the three rebars to three iron angles in each corner of the frame with the lashing wire. Put the angles 50 cm, 115 cm, and 180 cm above the ground marks.

18 Grip one iron at a time and push it down into the ground. Do a little at a time and alternating between the different irons. The tape marks show how far down the irons should go.

19 Measure both horizontally and vertically so that the vault is straight.

20 Remove the lashing wire tie and weld the brackets with the angles. Tap off the slag and check the welds. Plant a climbing plant in each corner to cover the arch in greenery.

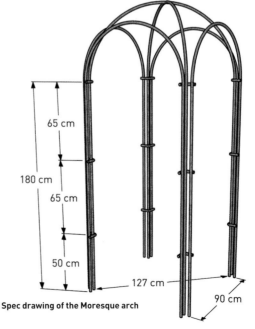

65 cm

180 cm

65 cm

50 cm

127 cm

90 cm

Spec drawing of the Moresque arch

FLOATING TABLE

Our white-painted, cast-iron furniture from Byarum is a favorite in the garden with its beautiful, classical forms. Since it is heavy to move, it has gained a permanent place of honor on the lawn under the old apple tree. Small and light furniture is also needed in the garden.

As a point of contrast, a small, light floating table made of slate and iron will be an exciting feature in the garden. To move the table, simply detach it from its hanging chain.

MATERIALS

- 1 slate tile (40 x 40 cm)
- 1 piece of plywood (35 x 35 cm)
- 1 round steel rod 2.3 m (8 mm)
- 1 heavy chain for suspension

TOOLS

- Tape measure
- Large calipers or pen and string
- Angle with cutting disc for stone
- Jigsaw
- Bolt cutter
- 2 iron pipes 1 m (inner diameter approx. 10 mm)
- 3 clamps
- 1 long screw clamp (40 cm)
- Drill
- Hole saw (41 mm)
- Bending machine or vise and pipe wrench
- Welder, e.g. a stud welder
- Chipping hammer

PLANTS

- Large flowered climber rose, *Rosa* 'Ilse Krohn Superior'

STEP BY STEP

The big hook for the floating table can be easily made in a bending machine. If you do not have access to one, you can fasten the iron in a vise and bend it with a pipe wrench.

1 Draw a circle on the slate tile that is 35 cm in diameter (see page 230). Cut the circle with an angle grinder.

2 Draw and cut a circle of 31.5 cm in diameter from the plywood board. The round bar should be bent with a length of 113 cm so that it makes one lap around the template with a remaining length of 14 cm. Mark the starting point on the circumference of the circle. Measure 14 cm from the starting point. Mark the end point.

3 Fasten the circle template with clamps along the workbench's edge. Cut a 1.8 m-long round bar, mark the 113 cm-point with tape. Insert the rod into the two iron pipes and place it along the edge of the table.

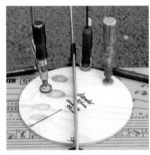

4 Fasten the rod at the tape mark. Use the iron pipes as handles. Start by bending the rod's long part gently around the template. Release the screw clamps, and advance the rod a little bit before it is clamped and bent further.

5 Drill three holes in the bending template when you have come so far so that the iron pipe is no longer to be used as a handle. Put clamps in the holes and fasten the rod to the template edge with clamps so that the rod end also bends.

6 Remove the rod from the bending template when the rod has been bent all the way to the final mark at 113 cm. The rod then opens and forms a circle 35 cm in diameter.

7 Bend the remaining iron rod at a 90-degree angle to become the suspension bar. Try the slate in the iron ring to ensure that it fits. Otherwise, adjust by pressing together or pulling the iron ring open.

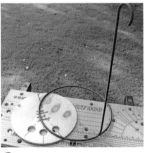

8 Bend a nice round hook with a diameter of 7 cm at the end of the suspension rod. This is most easily done in a bending machine.

9 Weld two round bars onto the bottom of the ring that is holding the slate. Put them 20 cm apart from each other. Weld the ring to the bent suspension rod.

10 Bend the rod so that the hook is centered over the table. Add the slate and hang the table in a heavy chain. Check that it hangs horizontally. Otherwise, adjust the angle of the rod.

PEDESTAL STAND

When raised above ground level and placed on a pedestal, a plant can become even more striking. Here, I have combined my two favorite materials, metal and concrete. This simple steel frame is made to fit the concrete slab with lace on page 69. The pedestal is charming and stylish, and it is stable enough to withstand strong winds. If you leave the steel untreated, it will begin to rust, giving the steel a natural, discreet appearance in the middle of the garden.

MATERIALS

For the stand supporting a small pedestal slab (29 x 29 cm) on page 69.

- 4.2 m precision square steel tubes (15 x 15 x 1.5 mm)
- 80 cm round steel rod (8 mm)
- One piece of plywood (22 x 22 cm)

TOOLS

- Ruler
- Hacksaw
- Metal file
- Cord
- Quick clamps
- Welding aggregates, e.g. stud welding
- Wire brush
- Chipping hammer
- Magnetic holders

Other Pedestal Slabs

You can use the stand for pedestal slabs made using materials or methods. However, always make sure that the disc has four 8 mm-thick dowel pins. For the small stand, the pins are positioned with a c/c (ie, center to center) distance of 20.5 cm. For the larger stand, use a c/c distance of 23.5 cm.

STEP BY STEP

The following describes how to make a small steel frame that will support a disc with the dimensions 29 x 29 cm. The sketch here also shows the large frame that supports a disc with the dimensions 33 x 33 cm. Both discs are manufactured in the same way but the larger one requires a 4.9 m steel tube, a 90 cm rod, and a piece of plywood that is 25 x 25 cm.

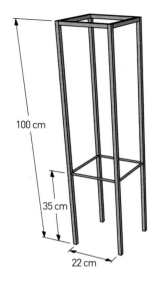
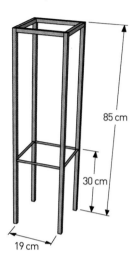

Spec drawing for a large and small pedestal stand

100 cm

35 cm

22 cm

85 cm

30 cm

19 cm

1 Cut the pedestal legs from the square steel tubes. The legs should be 85 cm long. Put the pedestal disc upside down and slide the tubes onto the disc's pins. Then cut the frame pieces to be about 19 cm long. Measure the distance between the legs before the frame pieces are cut.

2 Make a template from the plywood board. Cut out 1.5 x 1.5 cm pieces for the legs in each corner. The template is used to keep the legs parallel when welding. Put the disc between the bottom of the legs and tie the legs together with a string.

3 Keep the pedestal's legs together with clamps if they feel unsteady. A magnetic holder helps to keep the portions at a 90-degree angle. Brush off any rust with a wire brush and weld the frame parts to the legs.

4 Tap off the slag and check the welds.

5 Cut 4 x 19 cm long pieces of rod. Weld a rod between each pair of legs, 30 cm from the bottom of the hem.

6 Righten the pedestal stand and place it on a firm surface.

7 Place the concrete slab on top and fit it into the corner holes in the legs. With the slab in place, the pedestal is finished.

DECORATIVE TREE TRUNK PROTECTION

Anyone who has a garden knows it's not only humans who enjoy plants. Deer unashamedly eat flowers and rub their antlers against young shrubs and trees. Magnolia, cherry, and Euonymus are plants that are particularly attractive to the deer. When you plant a new tree, you should take measures to protect it to allow it to grow unharmed. I welded a protective fence for my newly planted tree, which also helps shape the tree as it grows. The fence is made in two halves that fit together with a simple steel loop over an adjacent brace.

Give the Bushes Some Space

Animals go after trees and shrubs alike. Often, shrubs that are attacked by animals perish before they have the chance to mature and flourish. For shrubs, use the same technique in welding the tree trunk protector, but adapt its shape to the bushes.

MATERIALS

- 12.6 m steel rod (6 mm)
- 2.4 m flat steel bar (12 x 3 mm)
- 1 steel chain with at least two links (internal dimensions approx. 7 x 14 mm) or 20 cm lashing wire

TOOLS

- Ruler
- Bolt cutter
- Bending machine
- 4 small clamps
- Welding aggregate, e.g. stud welding
- Wire brush
- Chipping hammer

PLANTS

- Cherry plums, *Prunus cerasifera*

Prunus cerasifera

STEP BY STEP

This trunk protector is suitable for a small ornamental tree where the crown branches begin at an approximate height of 70 cm. If your tree has a taller trunk, make the round bars longer to fit the tree.

1 Cut the round rod and flat rod with a bolt cutter. For the trunk protector the following materials are needed:
• 8 round bars at 1.2 m
• 6 round rods of 0.5 m
• 4 flats of 0.3 m
• 2 flats of 0.6 m

2 First, bend the long round bars for the standing portion of the trunk protector at a 10-degree angle, 50 cm from the edge. Then bend the short flat bars at an angle of 60 degrees, 10 cm in from each edge as shown.

3 To make the long flat bars tight against the standing portion, they must first be bent at a 10-degree angle, 20 cm from each edge as illustrated. Then, bend the rods at a 60-degree angle at the same place, but standing as shown in the previous image.

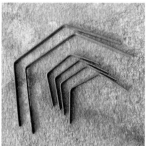

4 The six bent flat bars are completed. They will be the horizontal supports at the base of the trunk protector.

5 Place two of the small bent flat bars against each other on the lawn. Insert the eight long round bars in the soil as illustrated.

6 Angle the rods so that they stand straight and are symmetrically distributed. Adjust the height so that their angles are equal.

7 Fasten the other two small flat rods with clamps just below the bend.

8 Weld the upper part of the flat rods against the four rods on each half of the trunk protector.

9 Tap regularly to remove the slag with a slag hammer and check the welds.

10 Weld the two upper flat rods 10 cm from the top. Also weld the six short standing round bars between each rod so that the upper part of the protector becomes denser (see diagram to the right).

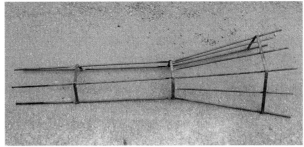

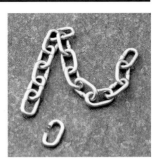

11 Turn the trunk protector upside down. Attach the lower small flat rods, 30 cm from the protector's bottom and weld them.

12 The two halves of the trunk protector are completed.

13 Cut off two links from the chain with a bolt cutter. The loose links become a stylish and simple lock to the trunk protector.

14 Plant the plum tree. The flowers have pink petals with dark red leaves. Hardy to zone 3.

15 Insert one side of the trunk protector on each side of the trunk so that the outer legs are touching each other. Attach the halves to each other by threading the chain links over the adjacent bars.

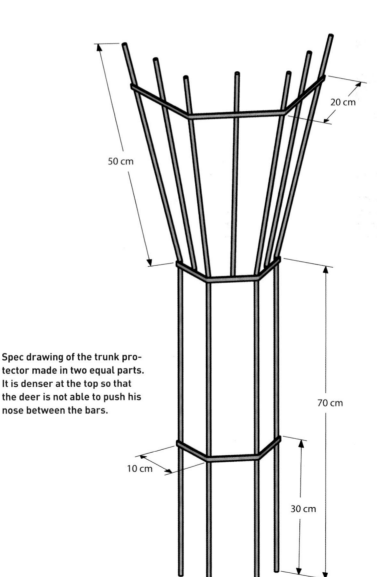

Spec drawing of the trunk protector made in two equal parts. It is denser at the top so that the deer is not able to push his nose between the bars.

20 cm

50 cm

70 cm

10 cm

30 cm

OUTDOOR CANDLE HOLDER

MATERIALS

- 4.9 m square bar of steel (8 x 8 mm)
- 2.8 m reinforcing steel Bi40
- 1 sheet of iron (5.5 x 146 x 280 mm)
- 6 liters of decorative stone ($^{50}/_{120}$)

TOOLS

- Compasses
- Ruler
- Scissors
- Ruler
- Angle grinder with cutting wheel for metal
- Metal file
- 3 welding tongs, type C-clamp
- Welding aggregate, such as stud welding
- Wire brush
- Chipping hammer
- Bolt cutter
- Magnetic holders

What is warmer and more welcoming than torches burning at dusk, during the dark winter? You could even place several of them in a row to light up the pathway and the entrance. To protect the grass, it is good to elevate the candles. For this, the holders should stand steady without falling over. Filling the holder with sauna stones helps to stabilize it and give it charm. When not being used for candles, the holder can support a hanging potted fuchsia.

Fold a Pentagon

Start with a strip of paper that is 85.6 mm wide and 680 mm long. Make a simple knot in the middle of the paper strip. Pull the strip tight so that it does not have gaps in the corners. Press the lines of the paper so that it forms discernible edges. Fold in the two bits that stick out and the pentagon is completed.

Polygon

STEP BY STEP

The candle holder is built with two iron plates with five corners that lie on a frame. Be sure to measure the frame parts so that it forms a regular pentagon.

1 Draw a pentagon with 9 cm-long sides on a piece of paper (see below and to the right). Cut and draw 2 pentagons on the iron plate.

2 Cut out the pentagons with an angle grinder. One plate should be the base and the second the top piece. Sand any sharp edges with a metal file.

3 Draw a pentagon on the welding surface. It must be 4 mm larger all around compared to the cut out pentagon. This will be the template for the base frame.

4 The frame is built from a square bar. Cut the rod into five 96 mm-long pieces with angled cuts. For a perfect pentagon the angles should be 54 degrees each (see sketch above), but it is also possible to cut freehand with angles around 45 degrees, and to fill the gap with a weld joint. Cut one piece at a time and check the fit against the template (step 6) before the next piece is cut.

96 mm — 54°

5 Align the frame pieces, one by one, to the template on the welding surface. The template shows the frame's outer edge. Adjust the pieces with the grinder if they do not fit. Fasten the frame pieces to the base with welding tongs so that they lay still.

6 Weld the frame. Remove any slag with a hammer and check the welds. Make another frame in the same way.

7 Fasten one framework on top of one of the pentagons and weld the frame and plate together. Now the frame is attached to the base plate.

8 Cut off some of the corners on the base plate frame so an 8 mm-wide and straight edge is formed. Cut the square bar for the legs in 5 pieces that are 65 cm long. Grind off sharp edges with a metal file.

9 Put a square leg against one of the trimmed corners of the bottom plate frame. The frame should be facing down and the leg should stick out 20 cm below the bottom plate. Hold the leg with a magnetic holder. Weld the leg to the frame. Do the same with the other four legs.

10 Weld all five legs to the upper frame. It should be 7.5 cm below the square rods' top edge.

11 Cut the rebars into five 50 cm-long pieces. The protruding parts of the steel rods should be 7.5 cm on one side and 5 cm on the other side.

Spec drawing of the candle holder. The upper plate is removable so that the holder can be filled with decorative stones.

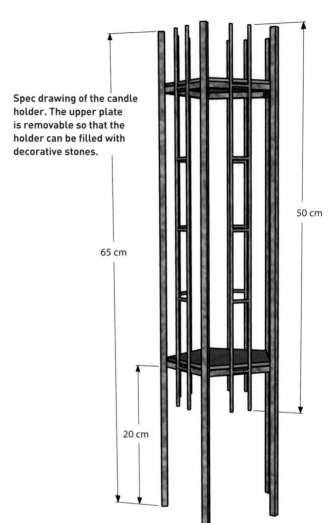

65 cm

50 cm

20 cm

12 Lastly, weld the rebar to the frames in the center of the pentagon's sides. The top of the reinforcement steel should be level with the top of the square legs.

13 Press the candle holder into the ground and fill it with stones. Finally, place the top plate on the top frame. Now the candleholder is ready. Enjoy!

Make a Perfect Pentagon

The proper name of an equiangular and equilateral pentagon is a regular convex pentagon. You can draw it geometrically. My pentagon is designed to be 10.4 cm in diameter, according to the size of my candle

The size of the pentagon is designed so that there is a 1 cm-space around the candle. The pentagon's sides become 9 cm long.

To do this:
1. Draw a circle with a radius of 76.5 mm.
2. Set the compass so that the radius becomes 90 mm. Place the compass needle somewhere on the initial circumference of the circle. This will be called point A and it will become one of corners in the pentagon. Draw a line that crosses the circumference of the original circle, point B. It will be the pentagon's second corner.
3. Move the compass' needle to point B and draw a new line that intersects the circumference of the original circle and creates point C.
4. Repeat until all five corners are marked.
5. Draw a straight line between two adjacent corner points, e.g. A–B.
6. Repeat for all neighboring vertices, and the pentagon is ready.

1.

2.

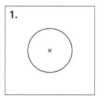

3.

4.

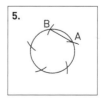

5.

6.

CHAPTER N°8

WORKING WITH GLASS

Shimmering glass

Glass is an incredibly fascinating and beautiful material. Since it lets light through, it can create stunning effects in the garden, especially when the stained glass reflects the sunlight to produce vibrant, intense colors. I use two different techniques to make the projects in this chapter. The basis of both techniques is to cut and join together different pieces of glass. In the first, I solder together copper-covered glass pieces to make a decorative plant support. In the second, the glass sheets are melted and shaped in a fusing oven to make a birdbath.

Light screens created with glass fusing technology by Charlotte Sjöblom Berg.

It's almost impossible to believe that magical, shiny glass can be created from sand, soda ash, and limestone. Glass even occurs in nature. During volcanic eruptions or when struck by lightning, the sand is heated so intensely that it vitrifies.

Generally, three components are needed to manufacture glass: a glass maker, a flux, and a stabilizer. Different eras used different materials for these three primary components. Back in 2000 BC, the Egyptians made glass objects using crushed mussel shells to extract calcium for the stabilizer. In the middle ages they used wood ash and marine algae.

Colored Glass

The glass gets its beautiful colors from small metal impurities. In the 1300s, the Venetians managed to remove the metal impurities in the glass, allowing them to produce colorless glass. Today, some metals or metal oxides are added in controlled forms for coloring glass in shifting hues. Cobalt gives the glass a beautiful blue color and chrome gives the glass a green hue.

Business and Pleasure

Glass's malleability and its unique ability to transmit light makes it ideal for window panes and electrical appliances. Plus, the beauty of colored glass is unparalleled. In the hands of a glass artist, sumptuous works of art can be made.

There are several different techniques for shaping the glass. Either you can work with hot glass (as they do in glass studios), or you can work with cold glass and glass fusing, lead mounting, and the Tiffany technique.

Lead Versus Copper

People have been making stained glass windows for centuries. From the start, stained glass windows adorned churches and chapels; however, with the beginning of the Art Nouveau period at the end of the nineteenth century, stained glass became a public art form and spread even to secular buildings.

It was during this period that Louis Comfort Tiffany, son of Charles Lewis Tiffany, the founder of Tiffany and Company, revolutionized the art of glass. He developed hues and patterns in the glass, put thin, flexible copper strips around the pieces of glass instead of the clumsier lead strips that were common, and merged the pieces together with a soldering iron.

The Tiffany technique allowed for more intricate mosaic patterns and complex two- and three-dimensional objects to be created. The products were also stronger than those made with the traditional lead bezel.

The Tiffany Technique

The Tiffany technique is also called "the copper foil technique." In order to create a glass piece following the Tiffany technique, you'll

This window screen by Eva Anundi is a beautiful and functional piece of art crafted with the Tiffany technique.

have to start from a Tiffany design. These are available for purchase, or you can create your own.

If you choose to create your own pattern, you'll need to draw the item you want to create full scale on a piece of paper. Then, divide the image into differently colored fields. There are special pattern scissors for cutting out the color fields and creating the piece templates. These scissors automatically remove a narrow strip of 0.8 mm to provide space for the copper foil. Remember that the color fields must be of a shape that the glass can feasibly be cut into.

Glue the templates to flat glass panels, and then cut out the pieces. Then, sand the edges so they fit together perfectly and tape a thin strip of copper foil around each edge.

Before soldering the pieces together, brush the copper foil with flux to prevent oxides from forming and to facilitate fusing.

If you want to keep the silvery color of the solder between the glass, you can treat the cooled solder with antioxidants so it doesn't oxidize in the air and darken.

Glass Fusing

Glass fusing is also called kiln-forming. The technique is based on stacking or layering pieces of cold glass and heating them in a kiln to roughly 800°C so that they merge. The method was used by the Egyptians thousands of years ago before it was supplanted by the more efficient glass-blowing method. In the middle of the twentieth century, the art regained popularity in the United States; since then, it has been further developed and interest continues to grow.

When fusing glass, it's important to use glass of the same type. Various glasses have different expansion coefficients. If you combine different varieties, stress fractures will appear in the glass when firing and the glass will crack when it is heated and as it cools.

Usually, the glass panels used are about 3 mm thick. When the glass is melted in the furnace, it will merge to become about 6 mm thick. If only one panel is used, the glass will shrink in the oven and when three pieces of glass are stacked on top of each other, the glass will flow out and lose its shape. Therefore, it's better to work mostly with two pieces of glass (each 3 mm thick); this way, when they are fused, the glass will maintain its original shape. To fuse the glass you need a kiln that can control the temperature and set a focal curve. The glass will first need to be softened at a lower temperature before it can be fused together. Then, it is cooled and relaxed in several stages before the fusing process is complete.

By heating the glass for various lengths of time you can create different effects. In a full fuse, the glass is melted together completely and the fused piece is completely flat. In a tack fuse, the glass edges become rounded and take on a softer shape, but the glass pieces retain their original form and do not melt into one another. After firing, it looks as if the pieces have been glued to each other.

You don't need to have your own kiln to fuse glass. Many glass artists are willing to rent space in their kiln. In this case, prepare the glass pieces at home.

Slumping

Once the glass has been fused, it can be formed into various products such as bowls, plates, and candlesticks. This is called slumping. Place the glass over a mold and heat the glass at a lower temperature, about 720°C. By firing the glass, it will soften and sink *into* the mold without affecting the color pattern in the glass. When you let the glass piece fold down *over* the outside of a mold the process is called "draping."

Separator

To prevent the glass from sticking to the bottom of the kiln, some form of separator is needed. This can be sprayed, brushed, or sprinkled over the surface. Or instead of applying a separator, you can put the glass on thin ceramic fiber paper, which is more convenient. The paper is pulverized during the burning and the powder residue can easily be rinsed away afterward with water.

Slumping molds can be manufactured from clay (middle) or stainless steel. You can make your own molds with special ceraform tiles (right). Fiber paper (left) is used as an under-lay or as an insert.

Finishing

If the objects have sharp edges after they have been fired, grind the edges with a diamond abrasive sponge. You can also drill and engrave the glass.

In lead-mounted glass, the pieces are bonded with lead strips. The antique lead bonded glass window in the Storkyrkan, Stockholm's impressive cathedral, pictures Olaus Petri and St. Sigfrid. The artist Einar Forseth made the glass paintings.

To Cut Glass

To become skilled in glass cutting, it is necessary to work with the Tiffany technique and with glass fusing. Cutting glass is an art in itself and takes a bit of practice. Oil or water is needed to cut glass. In some glasscutters, there is a small container that automatically dispenses oil to the cutting wheel. Hold the glasscutter firmly with the tip pressed against the glass. Draw the glasscutter over the glass with steady pressure. If you press too lightly you won't hear anything. If you press too hard, it will make a crackling sound. You'll quickly learn what a perfect cut sounds like.

Cutting Coaster

You can cut glass on a table or a simple cutting board, but you'll have to be careful to brush off the glass shards between each cut. A practical option is to use a waffle grid surface. This is basically a plastic grid that effectively collects any glass shards; you can also clamp rulers and other helpful tools to it.

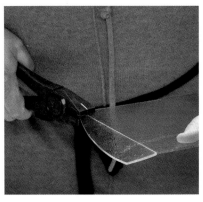

A straight cut is done against a ruler. Break the glass with wrecking pliers. The mark on the wrecking pliers should be placed directly above where you want the glass to break.

Curved lines are cut freehand. With the steel ball on the glass cutter, tap on the bottom of the cut line to make a notch along the cutting edge.

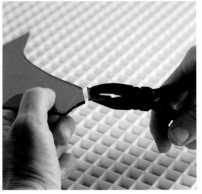

Curved lines should be carefully broken by hand or with a pair of small wrecking pliers.

SAFETY

If you're new to handling glass, it's easy to cut yourself on the sharp edges and small shards. Some people like to work with gloves that have rubber grips, while I prefer to work with my bare hands and keep band aids nearby just in case.

• Safety glasses are recommended for all glass cutting.

• Always use a respirator when handling powdered separator, processing form boards, and cleaning away the powder residue after firing ceramic fiber paper.

• Ensure good ventilation before soldering. The fumes should not be inhaled. If needed, place a small extraction fan near the soldering iron.

Different Types of Glass

There are many different suppliers of flat glass. Some glass is hand-made while others are machine made. The translucent glass is called "transparent." "Opaque" glass is, of course, not clear, and white opaque glass is called "opal glass." There is also glass with different effects. "Iridescent" and "favrile" glass have a unique sheen and look like there's an oily metal film on the glass. "Dichroic glass" has different colors depending on which way you look at it.

Using two-tone flat glass sheets for a dish can be very effective. This piece has black and transparent glass mixed.

Transparent glass in various shades of blue and green. Placing glass sheets of different colors on top of each other creates new colors—similar to painting with watercolors.

Glass Ornaments

With glass fusing, it is possible to decorate your creations in a variety of ways. Some types of metals—in the forms of wire, sheet, and plate—can be melted into the glass to produce different effects.

You can also paint on the glass before firing. The paint can be added between the glass sheets and on top of it.

Then there are various glass decorations like frits, noodles, stringers, and confetti. Frits are broken glass and noodles are glass rods 8 mm wide.

These spaghetti-like 1 mm thin glass rods are called stringers.

Confetti is paper-thin glass flakes.

GLASS APPLE PLANT SUPPORT

Some garden plants need a little extra care. Climbers will need something to climb on, fruit-laden branches may need a support to keep them from breaking under the weight, and tall perennials may need to be tied in place so they won't blow away in a heavy gust. Oftentimes, different plants can support one another in a natural and beautiful way. But sometimes a plant doesn't have a robust neighbor, and this is when we gardeners can lend a helping hand. A plant support can either be as unobtrusive as possible, so it doesn't take the focus away from the plant, or it can be an eye-catching garden decoration. This simple stained glass apple support glistens in the sunlight to immediately capture the onlooker's attention.

MATERIALS

The glass sheets are transparent and 3 mm thick.

- 1 plastic sheet protector (A4 size)
- 1 bright red glass sheet (65 x 95 mm)
- 1 dark red glass sheet (40 x 95 mm)
- 1 yellow glass sheet (15 x 45 mm)
- 1 brown glass sheet (5 x 25 mm)
- Glue stick for paper
- 3 sheets paper
- 75 cm copper foil (4.8 mm wide)
- Flux
- Solder
- 50 cm copper wire (0.8 mm)
- Dish soap
- Anti-oxidation spray
- 1 round steel rod 1.9 m (6 mm)
- 1 m wrapping wire
- 2 pieces of galvanized steel wire of 60 cm (0.7 mm)

TOOLS

- Scissors
- Glasscutters
- Glass wrecking pliers
- Brush
- Glass sander
- Lint-free cloth
- Plastic spatula or wooden butter knife
- Worktop to hold glass pieces when soldering
- Pushpins
- Soldering iron
- Round-nose pliers
- 20 cm sewer pipe (20 cm in diameter)
- Wire cutters

STEP BY STEP

The materials for the stained glass apple can be found at a hobby store or a specialized craft shop that sells material for glass work made with the Tiffany technique. The plant support isn't as fragile as it looks. It can withstand outdoor weather, but I will usually bring it into the greenhouse during the winter to protect it. After five winters, our stained glass apple is still intact and glittering.

1 Draw the pattern template (see next page) on a sheet of paper. This will be your original. Make two copies. Place one in a sheet protector; it will be used as a template. Take the second copy and cut out the individual pattern pieces.

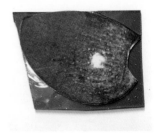

2 Glue the pattern stencils onto the glass sheets. Remember to place the stencils in such a way that you can cut out all the pieces without any problems.

3 Cut out each glass piece one at a time (see page 224). Brush off any glass splinters from the surface between each piece.

4 Grind the edges of each glass piece so they are smooth and so the pieces fit together perfectly. To do this, you'll need to regularly check the cut pieces against the template in the sheet protector.

5 Finish grinding all glass pieces.

6 Wash off any glue residue from the cut glass pieces. Wipe them with a lint-free cloth. Then, place the copper foil around the edges of the glass pieces. Try to center the foil as much as possible. Let the foil overlap a little at the starting/ending point.

7 Press out all the air bubbles from the copper foil with a plastic spatula; the foil should sit flat and be firmly attached to the glass.

8 Assemble the glass apple. If you're unsure how the pieces go together, consult your template.

9 Place the glass pieces on the work board and fix them in place with push-pins. Apply flux to the copper foil where the pieces are to be soldered together.

10 Heat the soldering iron and solder the glass pieces together. Make sure your workspace is well ventilated so you don't breathe in the fumes.

11 With round-nose pliers, form a loop of copper wire. Put the wire with the loop along the apple's edge.

12 Flux the thread and solder it against the upper edge of the glass.

13 Continue shaping the wire along the apple's edge and make another four loops evenly spaced around the rim. Flux and solder the wire as you go. Flux and tin the remaining copper foil and thread.

14 Wash off the remnants of flux with dish soap and lukewarm water. Rinse in clean water and wipe it dry.

15 Spray the stained glass apple with anti-oxidation spray (you may want to do this over a garbage can or outside). Be careful not to spray the floor; it can make the surface awfully slippery.

16 Polish the glass apple with a soft cloth.

The pattern for the glass apple is drawn at actual size. It consists of one stem piece and 4 apple pieces.

[Assembly]

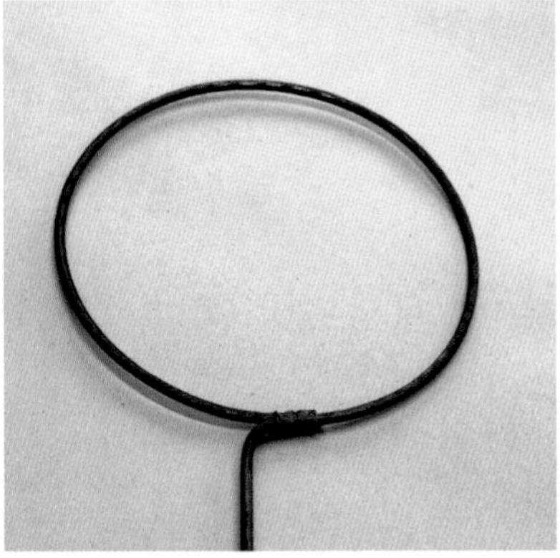

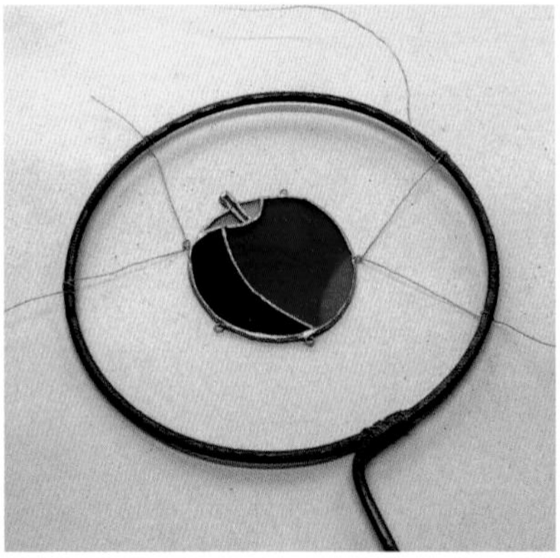

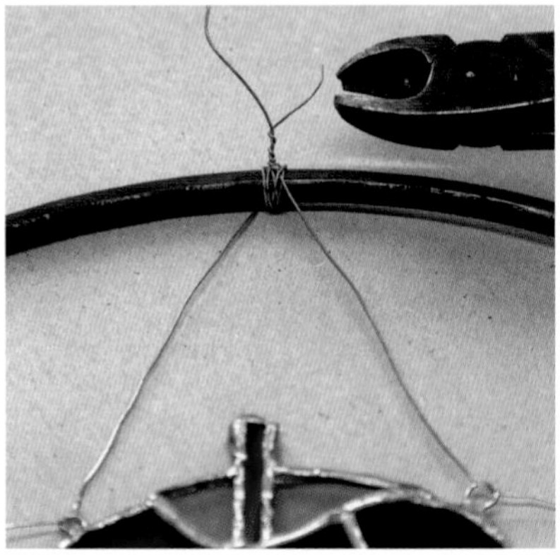

1 Form a round rod into a ring 25 cm in diameter. I bent it around a sewer pipe that was 20 cm in diameter and then shaped the ring until it was about 25 cm. You can also bend it around a tree trunk or any other round item. Let the round rod overlap about 2 cm at the end. Then, bend the round rod at a 90-degree angle to form a support pole. Tie the ring together with wrapping wire where the rod ends overlap.

2 Place the iron ring on a table and set the stained glass apple in the middle. Attach one of the galvanized steel wires by wrapping it 2–3 times around the rod. Thread the wire through one of apple's loops, and then bring the wire back to the iron ring and wrap it around. Do the same with the wire on the opposite side of the apple; this ensures that the apple will fall into the middle. Continue securing the apple with the steel wires. When it is finished, the wires should form a star around the apple.

3 Lastly, wind the wire ends around the iron ring and twist them together. Cut off the excess wire with a wire cutter. The plant support is now ready. Put it into the ground beside a plant that requires little additional bracing.

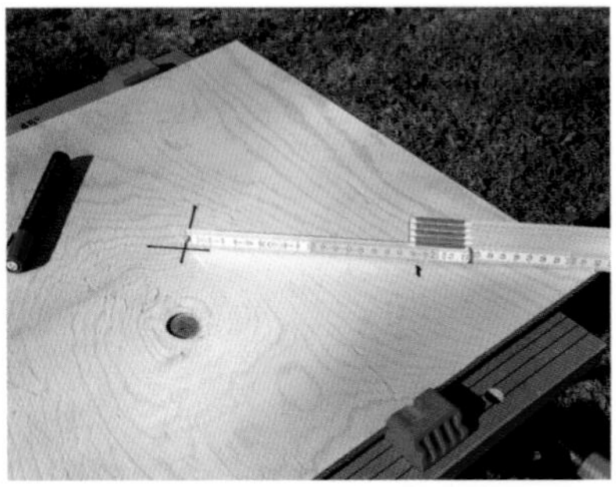

1

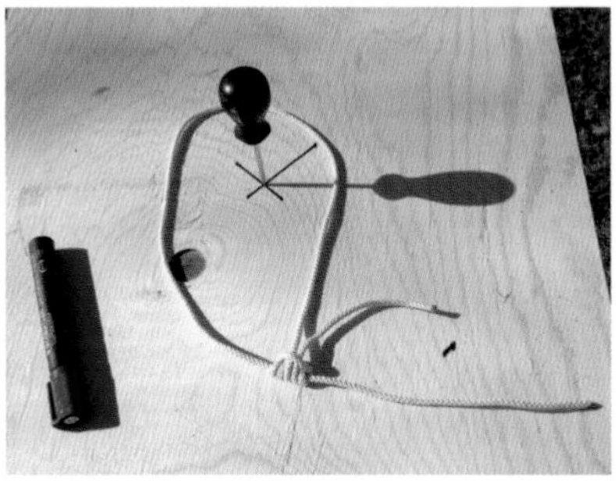

2

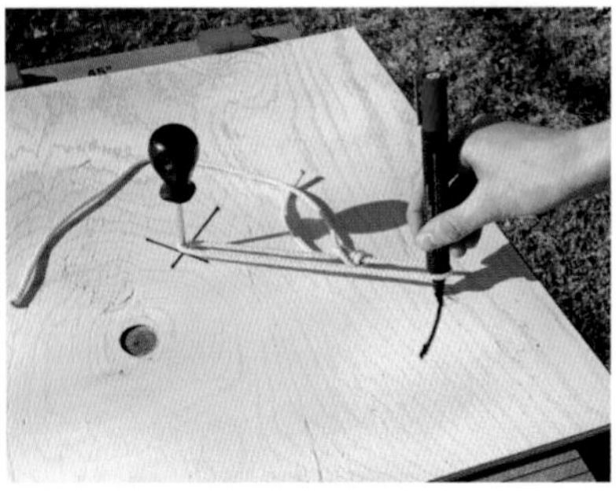

3

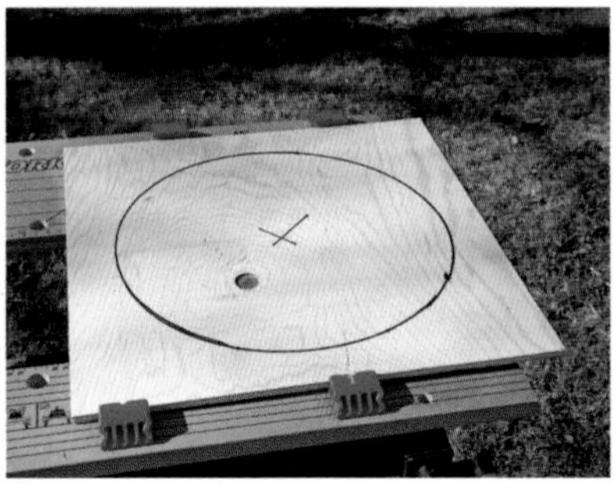

4

Drawing a Large Circle

For many templates, you'll need to draw a large circle. An easy and more exact way to do this is to use an awl or a nail, a piece of string, and a pen.

To do this:

1. Mark the center point of your circle and measure out the radius.

2. Stick an awl or a nail in the anticipated center point. Tie the string into a loop so that the length of the loop is equal to the circle's radius. Thread the loop over the awl.

3. If necessary, hold the awl in place with one hand. Put your pen in the loop of string and draw a circle with the string stretched taut. The string will guide your hand.

4. The circle is complete.

CITRUS SUPPORT

Doesn't the lemon tree have everything you can want in a plant? The beautiful white flowers emit a wonderful fragrance, and lemons grow over a long period of time to become large, mature, beautifully yellow, and extremely tasty! Even the shiny, somewhat harsh leaves have great ornamental value. With a lemon sapling, you get to enjoy this miracle for a long time, and it will carry leaves and flowers, small fruits, and ripe lemons simultaneously. My lemon tree needed a plant support. The three-dimensional stained glass lemon now supports the lemon tree's heavy, fruit-laden branches.

MATERIALS

The glass sheets are transparent and 3 mm thick.

- 1 plastic sheet protector (A4 size)
- 1 yellow glass sheet (160 x 110 mm)
- 1 green glass sheet (40 x 40 mm)
- 1 brown glass sheet (10 x 35 mm)
- Glue stick for paper
- 1.5 m copper foil (4.8 mm wide)
- Flux
- Solder
- 1 piece of copper wire of 12 cm (0.8 mm)
- Dish soap
- Anti-oxidation spray
- 1 round steel rod 1.1 m (8 mm)

GEAR

- Scissors
- Glasscutter
- Glass wrecking pliers
- Brush
- Glass sander
- Lint-free cloth, such as a linen towel
- Plastic spatula or wooden butter knife
- Worktop (for attaching glass pieces to be soldered)
- Pushpins
- Soldering iron
- Wire cutters
- Metal file

STEP BY STEP

The three-dimensional stained glass lemon has an outlet in the bottom that enables it to be stood up on a round rod. The lemon can easily be lifted off and moved around to different support posts.

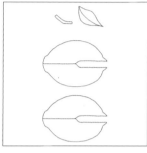

1 Copy the pattern for the lemon onto a sheet of paper (see next page). This will be your original. Make two copies of the paper template. Put one copy in the sheet protector; it will be used as a template. Cut out the pattern pieces from the second copy.

2 Glue the pattern stencils onto the corresponding colored glass sheets. Remember to place the pieces on the glass in such a way that you can cut all pieces without any problems.

3 Cut out each glass piece. Hold the glass steady. Be sure to hold the glass cutter upright, and make a cut along the edge of the stencil.

4 Tap gently on the underside of the cut with the glass cutter's steel ball to break the glass. Learn more about alternate ways to divide glass on page 224.

5 Brush off any glass shards from the workspace before cutting the next piece. Continue cutting out the glass along the stencils until all pieces are done.

6 Sand the edges of each glass piece so they are smooth and so the pieces fit together perfectly. The easiest way to make sure they fit is to check the cut pieces against the template regularly.

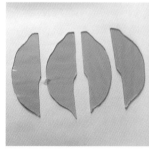

7 Wash off any glue residue from the glass pieces and wipe them dry with a lint-free cloth.

8 Place the copper foil around the edges of the pieces. Try to center the copper foil as much as possible. Let the foil overlap a little at the starting/end point.

9 Press out all the air pockets from the copper foil with a plastic spatula; the foil should sit flat and be properly attached to the glass.

10 Align two lemon halves on your worktop. Apply flux to the copper foil where the pieces are to be soldered together.

11 Heat the soldering iron and solder together the two glass lemon halves. Be sure your workspace is properly ventilated so you don't breathe in the fumes.

12 Take the third glass lemon half and apply flux to the copper foil where it is to be soldered to the first full lemon. Keep it perpendicular to the previous line of solder and solder it. On the opposite side, flux and solder the fourth glass lemon half.

13 Take the two pieces for the leaf and align them on the worksheet. Use pushpins to hold them in place. Flux the copper foil and solder the leaf pieces together.

14 Flux and solder the lemon's stem. Flux and solder a copper wire that will run between two halves of the lemon, about 1 cm from the stem. This will support the leaf. Insert the leaf so it rests against the support wire and the stem. Flux and solder the leaf at the two connection points.

15 Bend a support ring out of copper wire; the ring should be about 20 mm in diameter. Flux and solder the ring to the bottom of the lemon. Flux and tin the copper foil and thread that has not yet been tinned.

16 Let the stained glass lemon cool. Wash it with dish soap and lukewarm water. Use an old toothbrush to reach the cramped spaces so all the flux residue gets washed away. Rinse in clean water and wipe dry.

17 Spray all the solder seams with anti-oxidation spray over a trashcan or outside. Be careful not to spray any other surface or it will become very slippery.

18 Wipe off any excess anti-oxidation spray and polish the stained glass lemon with a soft cloth.

19 Insert a round rod into the space at the bottom of the lemon. It may require some adjustments, like sanding off some of the top of the rod, if it's too large. The citrus support is now ready. It can be stuck into a pot for a decoration, or it can be placed beside a plant in need of a support.

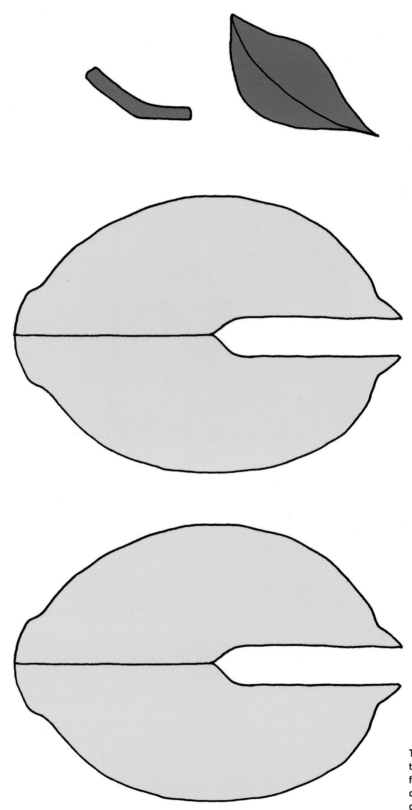

The stencil pattern for the lemon is made at full size and consists of four lemon halves, one stem, and two leaf pieces.

ORNAMENTAL TILE FOR THE TRELLIS

Large metal netting is incredibly practical and useful to have in the garden. The nets are light and airy in appearance and make a perfect climbing frame for climber plants. If the nets are left untreated, they will eventually become a lovely rusty brown. You can also paint them with a paint intended for metal surfaces, and in this way you can create an entirely different and expressive appearance (see page 103). In late summer and fall, the reinforcing networks are hidden by vegetation, but in spring and early summer they may feel naked. With a few decorative glass tiles, the net becomes a beautiful installation even during seasons that lack greenery.

MATERIALS

The glass sheets are transparent and 3 mm thick.

- 1 colorless base glass sheet (125 x 125 mm)
- 1 red glass sheet (120 x 120 mm)
- Dish soap
- 3 pieces of black glass scraps
- 3 stringers of 45 cm (in various sizes)
- 1 pinch of crushed glass (medium, white opal)
- Restraint glue
- 1 fiber paper (2 x 5 x 150 mm)
- 1 thin fiber paper (150 x 150 mm)
- 1 m galvanized steel wire (1.5 mm)

TOOLS

- Ruler
- Glass cutters
- Glass wrecking pliers
- Brush
- Tweezers
- Glass sander
- Lint-free cloth; e.g. a linen towel
- Scissors
- Kiln
- Wire cutters
- Round-nose pliers

STEP BY STEP

Material for glass fusing can be bought at hobby stores or specialized craft shops. When making decorative patterns, glass left over from previous projects can be put to good use. If you plan on renting space in a glass artist's kiln, prepare your decorative tile at home. The waffle cutting board shown in the photos below is a great buy, because it can effectively catch broken glass. You can even cut glass on a flat table, but you have to be careful to brush the broken glass away after every cut.

1 Cut a piece of color-less glass for the base; it should be 12.5 x 12.5 cm. Hold the glass cutter upright and apply a steady pressure. Tap the glass under the cut with the steel ball on the glass cutter; the glass should break off.

2 Assemble the pattern on the red sheet of glass, and play with the design until you are satisfied. I used left over black glass, and thin black, white, and yellow glass rods, called stringers.

3 Cut the red glass to be 5 mm smaller than the glass base, i.e. 12 x 12 cm. Grind the glass piece's edges so they are not rough.

4 Wash all the glass pieces with dish soap and lukewarm water. Rinse with clean water. Wipe dry with a lint-free cloth.

5 Cut 2 strips of fiber paper, 5 mm wide and 15 cm long. Place them on parallel sides of the base plate, 2.5 cm from the edge. Put the red glass sheet on top and position the decorative glass pieces the way you want them. The fiber strips will retain their shape in the oven and will form channels in the glass to be used when hanging.

6 Glue the decorative pieces onto the red glass.

7 Decorate the glass with small glass shards. Even the crushed glass can be attached with glue.

8 Apply a thin sheet of fiber paper to the bottom of the kiln so the glass doesn't stick. Move the glass to the fiber paper. Run the full glass fusing program so the glass melts together. When the fused glass is cool, remove the fiber paper strips from the channels.

9 Cut the steel wire into four pieces each 25 cm long. Shape the ends of the wires into a hook.

10 Insert a wire through each channel so the hooks are at the bottom of the decorative tile.

11 Flip the glass tile over, so the backside faces upward. Secure the hooks to the glass's backside.

12 Hang the decorative tile in one of the squares in the metal net trellis by bending the steel wires around the iron bar.

 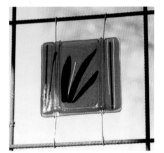

13 Thread the other two wires through the channels at the top of the glass tile. Secure the hooks around the decorative tile's top edge and bend the wires around the iron bar at the bottom of the square.

14 Cut off any excess wire and bend them around the iron bar so the stained glass sits tight. The stained glass can withstand rough weather and heavy wind and can be left on the trellis all year long.

More Designs

Here are some additional designs for decorative tiles. You can also drill holes in the glass for hanging instead of making channels.

BIRDBATH

A garden without animals is a lifeless spot. Though the deer that love to munch on your tulips and rosebuds may not be the most coveted visitors to your ornamental or functional garden, many small animals, birds, and insects are actually the gardener's friends. For example, the ladybug eats hundreds of aphids a day. The earthworm aerates and tirelessly improves the soil. If you're lucky enough to have a hedgehog living in your garden, it will eat both the earwigs and caterpillars. And little birds keep the pests at bay. Encourage the bird activity in your garden by setting out a stained glass birdbath—slightly above ground level and protected by vegetation—and it will attract visitors.

MATERIALS

FOR THE BIRDBATH
The glass sheets are 3 mm thick.

- 1 colorless glass sheet for the base (300 x 300 mm)
- 1 green glass sheet (250 x 300 mm)
- 2 blue glass sheets of different shades (130 x 270 mm)
- 1 black opaque glass sheet (70 x 70 mm)
- 1 white opal glass sheet (4 x 14 mm)

MATERIALS FOR FUSING
- Separator powder
- Slumping mold (30 x 30 cm)

TOOLS

- Ruler
- Glass cutters
- Glass wrecking pliers
- Brush
- Marker
- Glass sander
- Lint-free cloth; e.g. a linen towel
- Kiln

STEP BY STEP

You don't have to own a kiln to make a fused glass birdbath. You can often borrow molds and rent space in a glass studio's kiln. The mold for my bird bath was 30 x 30 cm, but see what molds the glass studio has so you can customize the dimensions of your glass to the shape. When I made the pattern I was thinking of a rushing stream. The black circle symbolizes a boulder on the bank of a stream.

1 Copy the pattern above at full size, 29 x 29 cm. Cut out the different pattern pieces.

2 Cut a piece of transparent glass for the base to 30 x 30 cm. I use a waffle grid, which catches the shards of broken glass. You can also cut the glass on a tabletop, but be careful to brush away the shards before cutting the next piece.

3 Start by cutting the pieces from the green glass.

4 If you have a large enough sheet of blue glass, the green pieces can be used as stencils for the shape of the stream. Place the green pieces on the blue glass so the outer dimensions match.

5 Use a marker to draw the wavy edges of the green pieces onto the blue glass. Place all the pattern stencils on the colored glass sheets. Cut the glass pieces out and check that they fit together properly.

6 Wash all glass pieces with dish soap and lukewarm water. Rinse in clean water. Wipe the glass dry with a lint-free cloth.

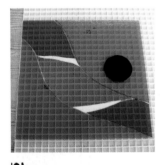

7 Grind the glass edges with the grinder to reduce roughness. Place the glass design on top of the base glass. The pieces don't need to fit together perfectly. The base glass will shine through any gaps in the color after the glass is fired.

8 Mix the separator with water and apply it to the bottom of the kiln according to the instructions on the bag. The separator will keep the glass from sticking to the kiln during the firing. Place the glass sheets in the oven and run the full fuse program so the glass fuses together.

9 Lastly, the fused glass sheet can be shaped into a bowl. Apply the separator to the slumping mold. Place the glass plate on top of the mold in the kiln. Run the slumping program so the glass softens and forms to the mold.

10 Place the birdbath in the garden or use it as a fruit bowl indoors.

The Color of the Sun and the Emperor

The sun may not actually be yellow, but sunshine is associated with a strong yellow color. In China, yellow was the color of the emperor because the emperor was descended from the holy sun. In America, yellow is perceived as a color of high energy and is often used to attract attention. Taxi cabs, ferries, and street signs are often yellow, and the yellow in a traffic light means you need to take extra caution.

Light of the wavelength 565–590 nm is yellow. Cadmium yellow is a classic color for artists and vegetable dyes such as saffron can produce yellow hues. Yellow flowers light up the garden from deliciously pale yellows to energetically bright hues. From early spring until late fall, they spread energy and joy.

Black-Eyed Susan, *Rudbeckia fulgida* var. *speciosa*

Fringed Tulip, *Tulipa* 'Hamilton'

Magnolia, *Magnolia* 'Elizabeth'

Winter Aconite, *Eranthis hyemalis*

Triumph Tulip, *Tulipa* 'Cherokee'

Buttercup Anemone, *Anemone ranunculoides*

Spring Pheasant's Eye, *Adonis vernalis*

Sunflower, *Helianthus annuus*

Knap Hill Azalea, *Rhododendron* 'Golden Eagle'

Climbing Rose, *Rosa* 'Leverkusen'

Yellow Day Lily, *Hemerocallis lilioasphodelus*

Yellow Foxglove, *Digitalis grandiflora*

Shrubby Cinquefoil, *Potentilla fruticosa*

Finding the right tools

It helps to have your own little toolbox that holds a tape measure and the most common tools. The more expensive equipment that appears in this book, as well as those that you'd only need to use once or twice, can be rented rather than bought. Sometimes it may seem tricky to pair the name of a tool with its appearance, therefore most of the tools and equipment that I use in the book's projects are illustrated in this chapter.

TOOLS

HAND TOOLS

1. Round-nose pliers
2. Needle-nose pliers
3. Cutting pliers, large
4. Cutting pliers, small
5. Pliers
6. Pincers
7. Pipe wrench
8. Bolt cutter
9. Hand riveter
10. Awl
11. Split needles
12. Shears
13. Round file
14. Flat file
15. Ratchet
16. Adjustable wrench
17. Wrench
18. Hacksaw
19. Axe
20. Chisel
21. Utility knife
22. Saw
23. Miter box
24. Sledge hammer, small
25. Sledge hammer, large
26. Hammer
27. Crowbar
28. Glue clamp
29. Bending machine
30. Quick clamp
31. Clamp
32. Iron stake
33. Spirit level, long
34. Spirit level, short

POWER TOOLS

35. Drill driver
36. Circular saw
37. Angle grinder
38. Jigsaw

◯ 1:5 scale

◯ 1:10 scale

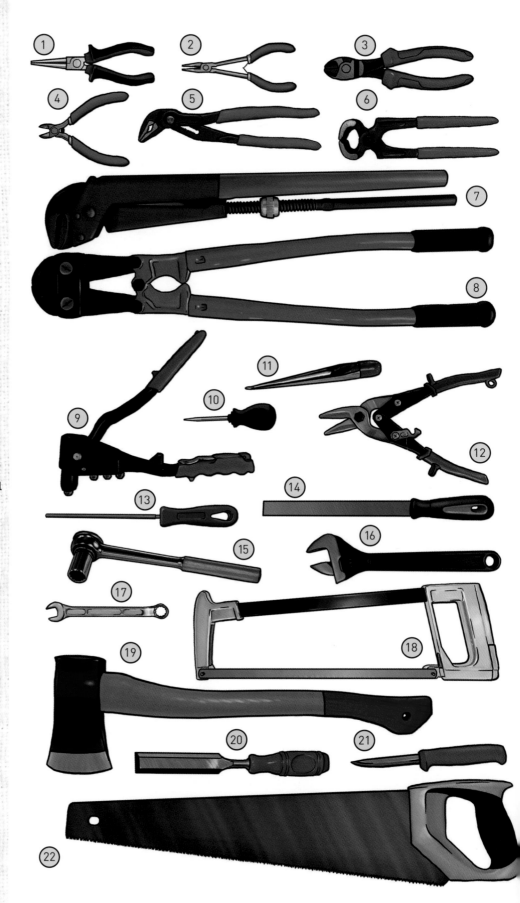

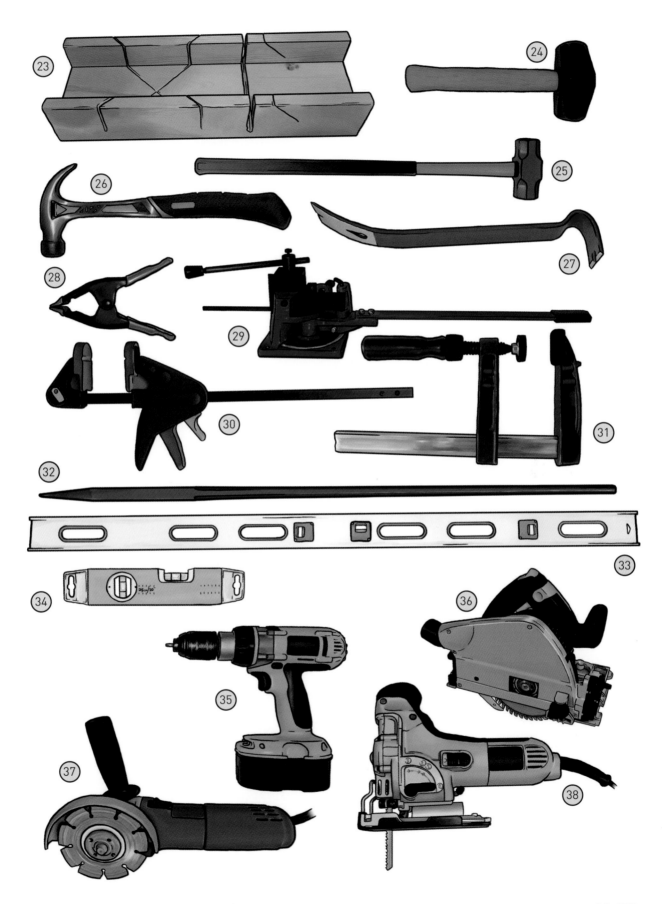

TOOLS

GARDENING TOOLS
39. Lopper
40. Pruning shears
41. Pruning saw

STONE & CONCRETE
42. Soil compactor
43. Mason's hammer
44. Chisel
45. Concrete mixer
46. Concrete mixing paddle
47. Rubber mallet
48. Notched trowel
49. Joint filler tool
50. Bricklaying trowel
51. Caulking trowel
52. Mosaic pliers

WELDING TOOLS
53. Welding machine
54. Welding clamp (C-clamp)
55. Magnetic holder
56. Welding/chipping hammer

GLASS
57. Glass cutter
58. Glass breaking pliers
59. Glass breaking pliers, small
60. Security bar
61. Soldering iron
62. Glass sander
63. Kiln

PROTECTIVE GEAR
64. Breathing protection
65. Goggles
66. Hearing protection
67. Extraction fan
68. Welding helmet

🔵 1:5 Scale

🔵 1:10 Scale

🔵 1:20 Scale

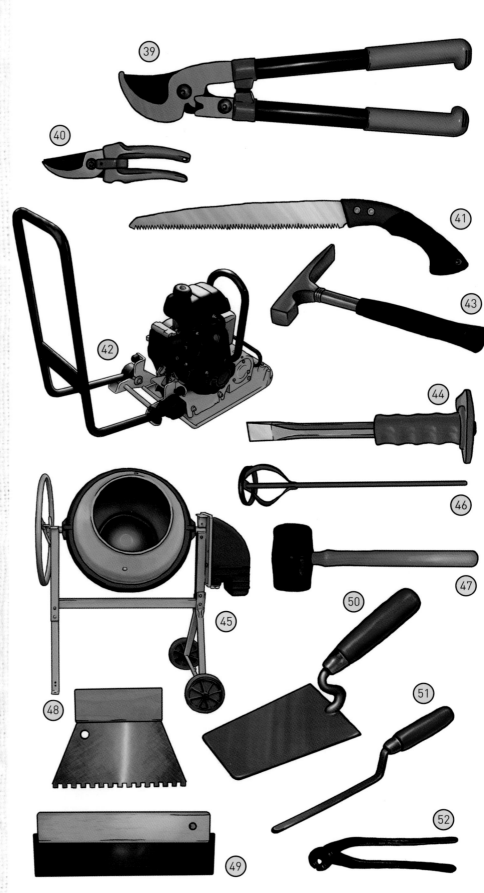

Acknowledgments

There are many of you who have helped me along the way of this, my first book.

A big thank you to my publisher Lisa Ydring, who accepted my idea and who supported and encouraged me throughout the undertaking. Thanks Kai Ristilä for a lovely design and my editor Cecilia Bengtsson, who tirelessly challenged the text and helped me refine it.

But without my beloved family, this task would have been impossible. Thank you for all the help and support. Kjell, your photos and help with the sketches has been invaluable. Sofia, thank you for the wonderful illustrations of the tools.

Adrian and Rebecka, thank you for always being willing to stand in front of or behind the camera when my own two hands are not sufficient.

Last but not least a big thank you to my sister Monica, my neighbors, and my friends. Monica, Martin Fagerlind, and Solveig Rotbring, you have all helped with material. Torsten and Anne Margret Pihl lent their garden and Krister Lööf their plants to photography. Thank you Cecilia Byström and Eva Rönnblom. Cilla, you thought all the time about my idea and got me to dare to invest. Eva, your wisdom and your enthusiasm has helped me very much along the way.

Text Copyright © 2013 by Marianne Svärd Häggvik, www.heliconiagarden.se
Photography copyright © Marianne Svärd Häggvik and Kjell Häggvik
English Translation © 2014 by Skyhorse Publishing
First published in 2013 as *Stora boken om trädgårdsprojekt* by Marianne Svärd Häggvik, Bonnier Fakta, Sweden
Illustrations of tools © Sofia Häggvik
Other illustrations © Marianne Svärd Häggvik

Labels by sxc.hu
Page 7 photo, Caroline Andersson
Page 136 photo, sxc.hu
Page 12, Månporten, Christian Erlandsson, Pil & Anläggning
Graphic Design by Kai Ristilä

Skyhorse Publishing books may be purchased in bulk at special discounts for sales promotion, corporate gifts, fund-raising, or educational purposes. Special editions can also be created to specifications. For details, contact the Special Sales Department, Skyhorse Publishing, 307 West 36th Street, 11th Floor, New York, NY 10018 or info@skyhorsepublishing.com.

Skyhorse® and Skyhorse Publishing® are registered trademarks of Skyhorse Publishing, Inc.®, a Delaware corporation.
www.skyhorsepublishing.com

10 9 8 7 6 5 4 3 2 1

Library of Congress Cataloging-in-Publication Data is available on file.

ISBN: 978-1-62873-649-6

Printed in China

Conversions

Metric	Imperial
0,1 mm	3.9370 thou
1 mm	0.0394 inch
1 cm	0.3937 inch
1 dm	3.9370 inches
1 m	1.0936 yard
1 kg	2,2046 lbs
100 ml	3.3814 fl oz, US wet
1 liter	1.0567 quarts, US wet

Approximations

1 inch	$2^1/_2$ cm
12 inches	$30^1/_2$ cm
1 yard	1 m
2 lbs	1 kg
1 quart	1 liter, US wet
1 gallon	$3^3/_4$ liters, US wet
10 cm	4 inches
1 m	1 yard
1 kg	$2^1/_4$ lbs
4 liters	1 gallon, US wet
100 ml	$3^1/_2$ fl oz, US wet

Metric Relations

1 cm = 10 mm
1 dm = 10 cm
1 m = 10 dm

1 liter = 1000 ml